MW01632241

THE ENTREPRENEUR DENTIST

THE ENTREPRENEUR DENTIST

HOW TO EXIT YOUR DENTAL BUSINESS RICH

DR. JERRY LANIER, DDS, EXEC. MBA

Published by Greenleaf Book Group Press
Austin, Texas
www.gbgpress.com

Distributed by Greenleaf Book Group

For ordering information or special discounts for bulk purchases, please contact Greenleaf Book Group at PO Box 91869, Austin, TX 78709, 512.891.6100.

Design and composition by Greenleaf Book Group and Kim Lance
Cover design by Greenleaf Book Group and Kim Lance
Cover images: Mirror Tool: PashaIgnatov/iStock Collection/Thinkstock; Dollar Sign: abluecup/iStock Collection/Thinkstock

Publisher's Cataloging-in-Publication data is available.

Print ISBN: 978-1-62634-636-9

eBook ISBN: 978-1-62634-637-6

Part of the Tree Neutral® program, which offsets the number of trees consumed in the production and printing of this book by taking proactive steps, such as planting trees in direct proportion to the number of trees used: www.treeneutral.com

Printed in the United States of America on acid-free paper

19 20 21 22 23 24   10 9 8 7 6 5 4 3 2 1

First Edition

DEDICATION

I dedicate this book to my children. This book should teach you how to fish, just in case Dad doesn't leave you any fish. I truly believe that what you learn is so much more important than what I could leave you financially. You should be able to leverage my confidence gained through my shared experiences to accomplish anything you set your sights on.

Contents

Why I Decided to Write This Book

THIS BOOK IS SOMETHING I'VE WANTED TO DO FOR YEARS—to share what I think is a very exciting journey as an Entrepreneur Dentist. I couldn't finish it earlier because the journey wasn't finished, and there was no proof of success at a level that would convince my audience I had something worth sharing with them.

Now after the completion of my mission, and with proof of success in hand, I'm ready to divulge what most consider a mystery: how to use your business to get rich. Looking back on it now, it seems much easier than when I was going through all the roadblocks along the way. But being a dentist was such a blessing for me that it seems as though it was my destiny—as I consider all of my life experiences to have been.

Because so many people struggle with being successful at business, and because I seem to have figured a few things out, I'd like to share some of what I've been given. Some call it "paying it forward," while others call it "giving back," but whatever I do, I just think of it as my journey, which the Creator is laying out for me as I go. I really don't know—or even worry about—what it entails, because He's shown me that when I listen to that voice guiding me, I'm always okay.

All that said, it's also good to have wealth and knowledge when you retire and walk away. The last thing you want is to have to return to work in old age or depend on others to live. I also hear a lot of dentists talk about downsizing their lifestyle after retirement, and I didn't want to even consider that kind of thinking. My vision of retirement involves traveling, staying in fine hotels, using valet parking at fine restaurants: not worrying about how much I'm spending, because my money is making more money than I *can* spend. I know not everyone can or will live this way, but obviously you're interested in having more, living a lifestyle of your choosing, and exiting the game rich, so let's talk about making it happen.

I grew up poor, and now I'm retired and wealthy. My life is still about my family and friends. I'm still happy most of the time. I like the same foods. I don't have the same worries, especially about money. But even more important than my assets are the knowledge and confidence I gained by accepting the challenge to become more than what people expected of me. I also did it for my dad, who died at fifty-eight. It always seemed to me that he had dreams that went unfulfilled, and I wanted to accomplish a lot in business as a way of honoring him.

Dentistry is one of the greatest platforms for launching a viable business. So why not share what I've learned over my career that enabled me to join the one percent? This book is an attempt to simplify the steps that will virtually assure you financial success. I also want to share the reasons I did things the way I did, which I call "leveraging what you are given."

The clinical side of dentistry is a medical profession and has to be taken seriously on its own. But the business side can be seen as a game you're determined to win. Putting them together, you create a great patient experience while growing a business that can someday be exchanged on the open market—to the highest bidder.

If you can do this, if you follow my advice, you won't have to depend on your children to take care of you when you retire. You can put all that responsibility on a corporation you've created and built up to great value; I'll teach you to create value in your companies that will reflect the value in you. I encourage you to plot your journey before you start. Pull over to the side of the road and input the coordinates into your mental GPS—where you want to go and when you want to get there. Now, then, get back on the highway and be guided along the way by your goals and by what you've learned.

From my time back in college, I always said I'd love to be a teacher—I just don't want to stand in a classroom. This is my chance to teach what I love talking about: *entrepreneurship*. This book is a supplement to the videos, social media posts, and other content I've created to augment my teaching, and they're all for you.

Remember the words Jim Rohn shared from his mentor: "Profits are better than wages. With wages you can earn a living, with profits you can earn a fortune."[1] Happy reading and happy trails along the way to your exit!

1 Jim Rohn, *Jim Rohn Weekend Event: Excelling in the New Millennium* (CD) (Plano, TX: Jim Rohn International, 2001).

Introduction

I GREW UP ON A FARM IN THE EASTERN NORTH CAROLINA tobacco belt. My grandparents were sharecroppers who lived on a tobacco farm, but my father actually owned eighteen acres of land. With eleven kids, including me, living in a four-room house, we were definitely poor. But when you grow up poor, you don't know anything else, so it doesn't seem like a big deal. I remember that, at one point, we had a television with sound but no picture; when friends talked about their favorite shows, I could only talk about the parts I had heard.

Farming has always been a hard life, and ours was no exception. For most of my life, I never caught my dad, Dave, in bed in the morning, even on Sundays. As early as I got up, he was always up before me. Working hard was probably my earliest lesson. But he taught us to be responsible. When I was thirteen, Dave would have my eighteen-year-old brother use dynamite to blow up stumps to clear trees off the land. It was a different time.

Dave was a no-nonsense guy, but he only made it to the third grade and never had any real formal education, except in the army. Because of that, he really pushed school, and that meant my siblings and I had to work hard to get good grades. I had no idea I would ever go to college, but I studied well enough that I never had to repeat a grade. The only class I ever worked really hard in was high school biology, because the teacher was young and pretty (and it was the era of the miniskirt). I scored my first high school A in her class, and she motivated me to perform my best and helped lead me to dentistry.

But there were some other important lessons my dad taught me . . . before lung cancer took him. One was not to waste time. We lived about four miles from the nearest store, and when he would send us for something, he'd say, "Go in a haste, come at a pace, don't stay long at any place." So we ran, and even if we saw someone we knew, we didn't have time to say more than two words to them, because we knew Dad had the clock on us. It taught me about completing a mission on time: Speed became a part of my game.

The other thing I learned from my father was independence. He never had a nine-to-five job. He was a North Carolina "pulpwood man," someone who harvested pine trees for market; the term "pulp fiction" refers to novels printed on paper made from the pulp of such trees. He also raised pigs and helped the other farmers raise tobacco and corn. After a long day, he would come home at night; the other loggers would come by our home then, so he could sharpen their saw blades. Because not everybody could sharpen, this became his side hustle. The men would line up, smoke, drink coffee, and talk late into the night. It was the only social time I ever saw my father take.

He wasn't orthodox, but my father controlled his time. He didn't answer to anyone and determined how much money he made based on how hard he was willing to work. I liked that, and I determined that when I got older, I would be as independent as he was.

"Damn, I Don't Want to Be Here Twenty Years"

But I was never a great student, and after high school, I wasn't really thinking about college. Instead, after graduation, I went to work at a DuPont factory. It was a great-paying job, but I was working swing shifts, rotating from 8:00 a.m. to 4:00 p.m., then 4:00 p.m. to midnight, then midnight to

8:00 a.m. That was rough, but the mindless repetition of the jobs was worse. For a while, I worked on a yarn inspection machine, facing this spinning spool all day long. When guys told me with pride that they were about to hit twenty years at the factory, I was horrified.

I couldn't imagine spending my life in that place, getting a gold watch, and then sitting in a rocking chair until I died. That's when I said, "Damn, I don't want to be here twenty years."

Around that time, my sister, who was in college, invited me to come stay on campus with her boyfriend. There was a concert and lots of parties, and college started to look pretty good. At twenty years old, I ended up enrolling in North Carolina Central University in Durham, the HBCU (historically black colleges and universities) that my sister attended. My first year, however, was a monster. As I mentioned, I hadn't been a terrific student in high school, and hadn't taken any college prep courses, so I spent most of that year in remedial classes. I was also falling victim to the—ahem—college social scene. I was a kid fresh off the farm, and Durham was a black mecca. Top musical groups (such as Parliament-Funkadelic) would come through, and there were always parties. I was like a kid in a candy store.

Unfortunately, the workload was too much. I was ready to put myself on a bus back home when my sister stopped me. She was a senior, a chemistry major, and had worked hard to become a star student. She sat me down and said, "What are you going to do, Jerry? We have all of these younger siblings." She was going to be the first one to graduate college, and here I was fooling around. Then she started crying and said, "Jerry, you're blowing it for everybody behind you. You have an obligation to the ones behind you to set an example."

That took me aback. She and I weren't just going to college; we were showing our younger siblings that a better life—a life that didn't involve poverty and backbreaking farm labor—was possible. She didn't want me to let them down. I decided that I owed it not only to myself but also to my family to take college more seriously. I cut back my partying and started my sophomore year determined to make college work.

Dental School

In my junior year, dentistry caught my eye. Biology had been the one class I excelled in, so a medical career seemed the way to go. I didn't want to become a physician, because I didn't see the entrepreneurial side. But most of the dentists I knew back then had their own shingle, their own private business. After DuPont, I didn't ever want to work for anybody else again. I needed something that was mine. Dentistry offered that.

I had another motivation, too. My sister's best friend worked for a successful black dentist in town. He had a nice brick building that was elevated from the street, and his Jaguar was parked next to the building. I said to myself, "That's probably not a bad life."

I passed the Dental Admission Test and then got accepted to the Meharry Medical College School of Dentistry in Nashville. But before I went, these guys came around the NCCU campus, recruiting people for summer jobs. You would go around the country selling reference books door-to-door, what the kids today would call old-school selling.

I decided it was worth a try, and I went to Nashville for a week of training—which, to my amazement, included sessions with sales *giants*, including Zig Ziglar. I got a week of invaluable hands-on training in sales and marketing, and then went off and sold books. That summer changed my life. Not only did I learn about the importance of selling and marketing, but also I learned about confidence and persistence.

I got a lot of rejections, standing at people's front doors in my tie with a big smile on my face. But I told myself that I had to believe what I was doing would work. If I kept selling the right way, eventually I would make sales. And I did. It gave me confidence, which I still have. If you're going to be successful in this world, you've got to have a little bit of a swagger.

Building a Multimillion-Dollar Business

In 1983, I graduated from Meharry, but I didn't start my own practice. I'd gotten a scholarship with the U.S. Public Health Service, and when you do that, you owe the government four years of service after you graduate. So off I went to work in the St. Thomas housing projects of New Orleans. It was hard work: There was a line of people when I got there every morning, and when I left four years later, the line hadn't got any shorter.

I also had a side hustle: I moonlighted at a dental practice I'd bought in a tiny bayou town called Hammond, Louisiana, about an hour from New Orleans. Running that practice taught me a great deal, but that, plus my work in the housing projects, was exhausting. To make matters worse, one day the Ku Klux Klan had its annual march in Hammond, right outside of my office on Railroad Avenue! I said, "Aw, hell no." I wanted out of the practice, but I'd signed a lease with the dentist who sold it to me, and he didn't want to let me out.

After a lot of pleading, his lawyer finally let me out of the deal, and I learned another important lesson: *Never make a deal without your lawyer's advice*. With my U.S. Public Health Service commitment done, and my Hammond practice closed, I bought the equipment from the housing project office and started my own practice with it.

Exiting Rich

In 1991, I relocated to Los Angeles, where I worked for a while as an associate while I looked for the right opportunity. Then, in 1994, I saw that opportunity—specializing in pediatric dentistry—and opened my first Kids Dental Kare office.

It was a smart decision, as it turned out. *U.S. News and World Report* had ranked dentistry and orthodontics as the number one careers in America for three years running.[2] Dentistry still has an almost unlimited earning potential. In 1994, when I started Kids Dental Kare as a dental support organization (DSO), I did it to get around the law in California at the time, which only allowed a two-office maximum. But the DSO structure allowed me to see how much I could expand its platform.

Fast-forward to 2017: I had 14 offices, with about 130 employees and 25 associate dentists, and I was doing about $20 million a year in revenue. That year, with the help of a team of investment bankers, I was able to sell Kids Dental Kare to a strategic partner for the *exact* amount of money that I had written down during a Tony Robbins seminar five years earlier. At the time of my "liquidity event," my revenue was in the top three percent of all dentists in the profession. Even better, my buyer didn't ask me to stay on for a year to help with the transition. I was free! Now, I'm living the life of my dreams.

I'm not telling you any of this to boast. I'm a confident man, but I'm also a humble one, because I know how much God has blessed me. Not long after I sold my business, I read a book called *Walk Away Wealthy* by a financial advisor named Mark Tepper. The book advises business owners and entrepreneurs on how to prepare to sell their companies profitably and

---

2 Richard Gawel, "*US News & World Report* Names Dentistry the Best Healthcare Profession," *Dentistry Today*, January 17, 2018, http://www.dentistrytoday.com/news/todays-dental-news/item/2827-us-news-world-report-names-dentistry-the-best-healthcare-professiondd.

exit rich, and I thought, "I want to help other dentists do the same thing." I'm sharing my story because I want other dentists to enjoy the same level of success that I have. Listen, you deserve it!

Years ago, I promised myself that I would become a teacher and give back to some of the people who shaped my life. But I didn't want to be in a classroom; it's too limiting. Yet, with a book and the Internet, I can reach tens of thousands of dentists who need this information.

What Does Your GPS Say?

I'll bet that you had a vision when you got into dentistry, and I'll bet it wasn't to create a new job for yourself—one where you're working sixty hours a week, afraid to take a vacation, with so much money tied up in the business that if something goes wrong, you can lose everything you've built in weeks. That's not independence; that's servitude.

I've written this book because I want to share how I achieved so much after starting with so little. A big reason for my success was that, from the beginning, I had the mindset that I would build something valuable and sell it. I had a bigger vision than opening one practice. I planned from the beginning with the end in mind. Dentists who fail to exit do so because the exit is always an afterthought, something they'll get to "one of these days." A farmer doesn't raise his crops or livestock to keep forever, because they start to earn diminishing returns. Farmers are preparing them for the market. Why would *you* not get *your* business ready for the market? Why not have *that* as your business plan?

When I mentor developing Entrepreneur Dentists, I use the metaphor of a GPS system. What makes GPS so useful is that you can just plug in your destination, and it gives you turn-by-turn directions to get you where you want to go. In my Rolls-Royce, when I give the verbal command for GPS, it responds with "Destination Input Guidance System." I like that as the description of what it does. It guides you to the specific destination that you input into the system. But if you don't know your destination, you can't plan your route. You can't just say, "Take me to my destination"—you have no idea where you'll end up.

That's the situation a lot of dentists are in. They haven't thought about where they want this industry to take them, so they don't even know where they want to be when they're ready to walk away, much less how to get there. Where are you trying to go?

Do you want to operate a family business and pass it on to your children? Do you want to build a business and sell it to your associates or partners? This is the all-important question that everything else is built upon: Your plans, your model or platform, and your strategic and tactical objectives all depend on you defining the destination, which should be your exit.

I wrote this book to help you benefit from my hard-won experience and leverage the incredible potential of this industry to build the wealth and future you want. You deserve a lifestyle deliberately designed by you to be everything you ever dreamed of.

If you want to exit rich, one of the most important shifts you can make is to start thinking not only like a dentist but also like an *entrepreneur*. Have a number in mind, a dollar figure you'd like to be able to walk away with at the end of your career. It's not all about the money, but in this game, it's the way we keep score.

Let's add to the scoreboard. How many offices will you have? How many employees? How many patients? How much revenue do you want to be bringing in each month? Once you know all this, you'll have your navigational target. Set your GPS toward it, and then you'll know what you're aiming for. Aim high. You'll work just as hard to reach a mediocre number, so go for it.

Study the industry. What specialties—pediatrics, orthodontics, extractions, cosmetic—are doing well and earning high multiples and sales prices? What are hedge fund managers and private equity funds buying into? Who are the industry leaders that might want to acquire your brand to add to their portfolio? What the heck is EBITDA?

We'll get to all that.

I want you to learn to think this way: *If your cash flow stops every time you stop working, you need a better plan*. Part of being an Entrepreneur Dentist is having your money work for you while you sleep. In his book *Cashflow Quadrant* (which I encourage you to read), Robert Kiyosaki talks about the four financial quadrants of an individual's working life:

1. **Employee**—You trade your time for money.
2. **Sole proprietor**—You work for money, but you're the owner.
3. **Business owner**—You own a business system where others work for your money.
4. **Investor**—Your money works for you.

My dental offices were the platform I needed to get into that fourth quadrant—the quadrant where real, long-term wealth becomes possible.[3] That's the quadrant I want you to aspire to.

---

3 Robert Kiyosaki, *Rich Dad's Cashflow Quadrant* (Plata Publishing, LLC, 2015).

What's in the Book?

Building a multimillion-dollar dental business is a complicated subject, and I have no illusions about covering all of it in a single book. Instead, I've tried to frame and organize what I've learned according to some important tools and processes.

- ***Stay in your lane.*** A man I met once—he called himself "Lucrative Larry"—said this to me. He meant focus on your specialty; don't try to be all things to all people. Find the niche work you're good at and know intimately and stick with it. He was right. I was in children's dentistry for thirty-three years and limited my practice to kids in the low-to-middle-income bracket. Most dentists strive to serve the wealthy, but the masses are the bulk of the market; and that's where the opportunity lies. It made me a rich man. That's why I say, "Your niche will make you rich." I'll explain how.

- ***Remember the five P's of building a saleable dental business.*** If you want to build something that will be of value to an investor, you can't think just as a dentist anymore. You need to think about the five *P*'s that will attract a buyer:

    1. **Product**—Something of value that the market wants;
    2. **Packaging**—A strong brand and a unique position in the market, differentiating you from everyone else;
    3. **Promotion**—Marketing is not a thing we do, it's everything we do;
    4. **Profits**—Buyers demand profitability and cash flow; and
    5. **Presentation**—A partner, probably an investment banker, to take the little piggy to market with style and put on a show that sells.

- ***Follow the GPS Process.*** If you don't know where you're going, who knows where you'll wind up? I'll teach you this simple process:
    1. Deliberately define your destination.
    2. Lock it into your internal GPS.
    3. Choose an estimated time of arrival (ETA).
    4. Devise your plan. Be as detailed as possible—but be ready to adjust.
    5. Get started *now*. A plan without action isn't worth the paper it's written on.
    6. Trust the plan and keep moving. Don't get distracted by things that don't get you closer to your destination.

Think, Do, Keep in Mind

To make this material easier to digest and use, I've roughly divided each chapter into three sections:

- **Think**—Productive attitudes, mindsets, and approaches;
- **Do**—Actions, policies, and processes I've found to be winners; and
- **Keep in Mind**—Warnings, important things to know, and mistakes I've made that you shouldn't.

I've also included some extra features:

- **Check Your GPS**—We'll check in at the beginning of each chapter to make sure you're on course with the GPS process.
- **Talk to the Expert**—In each chapter, experts will offer advice on the subject at hand, from finance to marketing to risk assessment.

- **Lucrative Larry Says**—Lucrative Larry was from the streets, but he knew a lot about business and gave me a lot to pass along.
- **Eyeing the Exit**—This is our sidebar discussion on things like branding, making yourself "obsolete," predictable cash flow, and more.

Becoming an Entrepreneur Dentist is about looking up from the daily grind (or handpiece) and planning for the future you want. As I tell my son, "Proper planning and preparation prevent poor performance." He plays piano and takes both classical and jazz classes, and sometimes he tries to fake it through a lesson. But you can't. Your performance will tell the story. If you haven't prepared and practiced, your performance will be poor. Your business prospects obey that same rule.

My hope is that reading this book will help you think like an entrepreneur, develop the confidence that you *can* do this, and figure out what you really want. If having a small office where you run everything and make a nice living is what makes you happy, do that. But I want to give you all the tools you'll need if you decide you want to exit rich.

That means thinking differently about money—about accounting, marketing, and hiring. It means viewing your business as something that can be automated and systemized so that it runs smoothly—so that you can grow your enterprise and your net worth. It means building the life you want intentionally and purposefully. Being a dentist is a great path to doing just that. Let's make it happen.

To your wealth . . .
Dr. Jerry Lanier, DDS

CHAPTER 1

The Best Profession to Make Money

CHECK YOUR GPS

You're just beginning your journey, so this is the time to make sure you've chosen a clear, appropriate destination.

- **Deliberately define your destination**: What do you want your post-work lifestyle to be? What amount (come up with an actual number) would you need to sell your dental business for in order to have that lifestyle?
- **Lock it into your internal GPS**: How big would your business need to be for you to get your price? Get an idea of what practices are selling for. This is a great time to talk to investment bankers and other dentists who've exited.
- **Choose an ETA**: Write down a rough idea of when you might want to sell your business. Pick a year that seems reasonable based on where you are now. For example, if you only have one office, you might be ten years out. If you have four to five, five years might be realistic.

continued

- » **Devise your plan**: Begin thinking about your brand, a niche that you could dominate, and a system that you could develop to help you run a larger business.
- » **Get started now**: Determine the steps you can take in the next thirty days. What could you do today that would put you closer to that *exit*?
- » **Trust the plan and keep moving.**

A while back, I came up with the acronym "BAD," which stands for broke-ass dentist. I thought about having t-shirts made until I realized that there was no point. There's no such thing as a broke-ass dentist. That's why I felt comfortable opening this book saying something provocative about how easy it is to make money caring for people's oral health.

There are middle-income dentists. There are upper-middle-class dentists. There are rich dentists. But you can't be an impoverished dentist unless you're incompetent or a criminal. *U.S. News and World Report* wrote that as of 2016, the average American dentist's salary was $172,860. If you're a specialist, the news is even better: In 2016, the average orthodontist earned $228,780, while the average oral and maxillofacial surgeon earned $232,870.[4] All three are comfortably in the top ten percent of American incomes.[5]

But that doesn't explain why it's so easy to make money in dentistry. After all, dental schools normally cost $200,000, with some private schools getting

---

4 Richard Gawel, "*US News & World Report* Names Dentistry the Best Healthcare Profession," *Dentistry Today*, January 17, 2018, http://www.dentistrytoday.com/news/todays-dental-news/item/2827-us-news-world-report-names-dentistry-the-best-healthcare-professiondd.

5 U.S. Census Bureau, "American Community Survey Five-Year Estimates," December 6, 2018, www.census.gov/programs-surveys/acs.

as high as $400,000 for four years of education. Based on my experience, a new dental office build-out, with equipment and everything else, could cost you between $450,000 and $1 million. That's heavy. How can dentistry be such a cash cow when you start your career with a crippling debt load?

Start with the fact that you can amortize those equipment purchases over a long time, maybe twenty years. True, just like an iPhone, your dental equipment will have to be upgraded to the latest model pretty regularly—but once you've got your dental business running, you'll have the cash flow to do that. And amortization is only one of the minor considerations explaining why dentistry is so profitable.

Here's one of the big ones: Dentists are among the most desirable customers for banks to lend to. It turns out that dental businesses almost never fail. According to the U.S. Small Business Administration (SBA), from 2006 to 2015 the ten-year loan default rate for dental offices was only 5.2 percent. For perspective, the average SBA default rate from 2006 to 2015 was 17.4 percent. It's no wonder dental offices are among the businesses with the highest SBA loan approval rates.[6]

So dentistry is stable and profitable, and demand is more predictable than anything except the funeral business. No wonder banks love us. Even better, because they see us as low risk, interest rates are low. That makes capital cheap and readily available, so it's easy for you as an Entrepreneur Dentist to add locations, grow your business, and increase your wealth. But I'll come back to that.

---

6 Kevin Voigt and Caren Weiner Campbell, "1 in 6 Small Business Administration Loans Fail, Study Finds," NerdWallet, October 3, 2017, www.nerdwallet.com/blog/small-business/study-1-in-6-sba-small-business-administration-loans-fail.

THINK

- **Your practice as product.**
- **Six reasons dentistry is so lucrative.**
- **Why you might not be making as much money as you should.**

Dentistry Is Like Pig Farming

You might already have noticed that I don't generally call it a dental *practice*. Instead, I refer to what I built—and what you're trying to build—as a dental *business*. That's intentional. When you start thinking of it as a business, you are more apt to learn how to operate it as a business. By referring to yourself as an entrepreneur, by definition, you are saying you are a businessperson.

Some dentists think it's sacrilege to consider dentistry a business, but you should be thinking of taking your little piggies to market. Back on the farm, they call it "topping out," because there's an optimal time for any livestock to be sold. In business, it's referred to as a liquidity event, but the principle is the same—and you should be aiming for it.

Imagine yourself as an entrepreneur, running a network of busy dental offices, all anchored by a strong brand, run by powerful enterprise management software, and managed by a team of handpicked pros you've worked with for years. Isn't that what you have in mind?

When you think of your career as building a business, not just building a practice, it changes the picture you have in your head. When you stop thinking of what you're doing as being a clinician and start thinking of yourself as building a brand and growing something that an investor will find valuable enough to buy, you will see your role in a different way.

You start taking the time to learn to read financial statements. You take business and marketing classes. You discover the value in paying for top-flight legal and tax advice. Your perspective goes to another level.

Most of the profit in dentistry today goes to someone who doesn't have a DDS. Why? Because that person is an entrepreneur with an MBA, someone who understands the numbers, the market forces, and the principles of demand and value. In reading this book, you're announcing that you're not in the dental business but the *value* business. Someone will buy your practice not because you've worked hard or because they admire dentistry, but because they see it as a good investment, and you've built something that delivers ROI.

Early on, I took a course created by Michael Gerber, the author and business skills–training expert. One thing he said sticks with me to this day: "Think of your business as your product."[7] My father took pigs to market; your business provides expert dentistry and oral care services. They're exactly the same thing. They're *products*.

The reason so many dentists work themselves to death or flop at building companies is that they don't think this way. They think calling dentistry a product is demeaning. But a product is just something you deliver that other people find valuable enough to pay for. Your knowledge of dental science is a product. Your great chairside manner that makes patients feel at ease? A product. Your relaxing office décor, convenient location, appointment reminders by text message, on-site fabrication of crowns and veneers—they're all your products.

If you think of them that way, and think of your goal as delivering value so consistently and efficiently that you become steadily profitable, you will create so much value that, one day, you'll be the one exiting rich.

---

7 M. E. Gerber, *The E-Myth Revisited: Why Most Small Businesses Don't Work and What to Do about It* (New York: HarperBusiness, 1995).

LUCRATIVE LARRY'S ADVICE ON . . . MEDICAID

Get over the taboo attached to Medicaid! Jerry did when he saw that fifty-one percent of children in California are covered by Medicaid. That's not a stigma; it's an opportunity.

Six Reasons Dentistry Is So Lucrative

If you've been looking at the big-ticket group practices and DSOs with envy while you slave away in your single office, you might be saying, "Dr. Lanier, how on earth can you claim that dentistry is an easy way to make money?" I never said it was an *easy* way to make money, because it's not. School, building your first office—it's hard work. No doubt about that.

What dentistry has that no other profession does is the potential for substantial, fast growth with very little resistance in the market. If you make good decisions from the beginning (more on that later), you can start hiring associates, opening new locations, and bringing in a lot of cash with surprising speed.

Why is dentistry so lucrative? Here are six reasons:

1. ***Dental care is a universal need.*** If you have teeth, you need to see us. If you don't have teeth, you really need to see us. It's part of American culture: You see your dentist every six months for a cleaning, and most of the time we're going to find something else that you need, from a filling to a crown. As people age, they need oral maintenance. That's just reality. That means there's a constant demand in any community, and if you don't satisfy it, someone else will. Even though

insurance doesn't cover 100 percent of the cost, most people are willing to pay the difference, as long as it's within reason. That alone is enough for a single office to bring in $75,000 a month and give you a nice standard of living.

2. ***People will always spend on dental care for their kids.*** One of the main reasons I chose pediatric dentistry as a niche is because even if parents won't see a dentist themselves, they'll spend money on dental care for their little ones. You don't have to run a pediatric-only business to benefit from this, either. Just make sure your office and people are kid-friendly, because if you can get the kids to love seeing you, you'll probably get Mom and Dad, too. But I find that you're either a kid's dentist or an adult dentist. So hire associates to do what you won't do—and promote them separately, so that you have a multi-specialty practice. Market it as such.

3. ***Even as a GP, you can limit your practice to a specialty.*** There is such a demand for general practitioners that you can limit your practice and focus on a specific segment of the population and do specialty work. My point here is that it's great to be able to do anything, but it's far better to limit what you do so that you're known for something. Don't try to be all things to all people; as a generalist, you can hire specialists, other generalists, hygienists, etc. Just make sure your brand is known for something, whether that's pediatrics, orthodontics, endodontics, or something else. Otherwise, you're a "JAD"—just another dentist.

4. ***Everyone knows and expects dentistry to be expensive.*** With the economy humming along, it's a great time to charge handsomely, if your market supports it. If you're in a high-end market, your prices

have to reflect your expenses, and you should spend on your facility to make patients feel comfortable with your fees.

5. ***Technology is making it easier.*** It's hard not to win with all of the resources available. Now there are lasers that can remove decay without anesthesia. We have chairside crowns and restoratives. We have orthodontic appliances that GPs can sell and deliver great results. It's easier to manage your offices using new enterprise systems.

6. ***There's an abundance of training available.*** DSO leaders, and organizations like the Association of Dental Support Organizations (ADSO) and the Dentist Entrepreneur Organization (DEO), are giving seminars regularly. There are mentoring videos and stories of others that have already blazed a trail for you to follow. It's easier than ever to learn how to grow your business. Now it's time to start the journey to your well-defined destination.

DO

- **See yourself as exceptional.**
- **Build a brand that communicates unique value.**
- **Be a little paranoid about your people.**

How to Build an Exceptional Business

But even with all those advantages, building an exceptional dental business is not easy. Being an entrepreneur never is, because there are endless pitfalls standing between you and your goals. I've found that one of the keys to overcoming those obstacles is seeing yourself as exceptional, too—not as just another run-of-the-mill dentist, but as someone who deserves better and has the skills to make it happen. Someone who's earned his or her GSD (gets sh*t done) degree. Confer one upon yourself after you're confident you've earned it.

A few years ago, I met someone who fit that bill. He was a former classmate of mine, and we were driving in L.A. and talking about business when he said, "I sold my practice, and now I work for one of these larger DSOs. I'm doing their implants, extractions, and dentures. I generate $1.8 million a year for them and I get thirty-five percent. This is the happiest I've ever been. I get paid all this money, and I go golfing almost every day."

That dentist is a success story—in part because he valued himself highly enough to create an exit path that makes him happy. He's phenomenally skilled and great with patients, so he can work when he wants and write his own ticket. But nobody gave him that. He demanded it and got it.

Too many dentists are passive about their futures. Here's a portrait of the typical dentist that I see. He (or she) looks tired all the time. He works six days a week, so he doesn't see his family. He feels stretched thin, but there never seems to be enough money. He's in debt. He's frustrated because he's trying to do everything himself, because he doesn't want to pay a lawyer, accountant, or IT professional. He has a vague idea of wanting to grow but never takes the time to figure out how that can happen, so year after year comes and goes, and he's still on the treadmill . . . with no end in sight. He looks at dentists who own prosperous multi-location dental businesses with jealousy, because they're living in Beverly Hills and buying boats, while he's doing just okay. He's exhausted and unhappy.

Do you see anything like that person when you look in the mirror? Now is the time to change things and make different choices. It doesn't matter if you've been practicing for ten years; it's never too late to get on the entrepreneurial path and start planning for a multimillion-dollar exit. But you have to start doing a few critical things differently:

» ***Focus or limit your practice.*** Focusing on pediatric dentistry was the best decision I ever made. Too many dentists try to do everything because they're afraid of losing business. But when you do that, the public will perceive you as just another general dentist who's an expert in nothing. Do what you enjoy and are good at. If you like doing implants, you can make a lot of money at that, so be the dentist in your area who specializes in implants. Refer out non-implant work to dentists who will refer implant patients to you. I'm not implying that you should do everything on a quid pro quo basis, but that it's smart to limit your work to what you do well, and to walk away from everything else. I know it's hard to turn away business, but owning a niche takes discipline.

Focusing on your particular niche will increase your value and status in the eyes of your patients. When I walked into the room to work with a child, I introduced myself: "I'm Dr. Lanier." If I noticed any kind of nervousness or trepidation in the child or the parent, I'd say, "Listen, you can relax. This is the only thing I do. I don't cut my grass, I don't do anything else. I only work on kids, and I'm really good at it. You can trust me on that." The effect on people was amazing.

The world doesn't need more jack-of-all-trades general dentists. They're the ones who will be pulled under as the industry consolidates. As you limit your brand, you can run a boutique business that serves markets the DSOs can't or won't, and you'll get referrals. But as you grow these practices, you want to become the target of an acquisition.

» ***Brand yourself.*** I cringe every time I drive by a dental practice in a strip mall with a sign that just says "Dentist." That's the equivalent of generic medication. It's a huge missed opportunity. That dentist isn't connecting with patients, pulling in walk-ins, or anything else. He or she is just another dentist.

My Kids Dental Kare locations—well, let's start with the name: Kids Dental Kare. I had a name that was memorable and instantly told everybody my specialty. I also had colorful, well-decorated offices, did lots of marketing, and had a strong community presence. I didn't just build a business, I built a brand. Kids Dental Kare stood out and told a story that people could relate to. You must do the same.

» ***Listen to the experts.*** I'm a well-trained, skilled dentist. I'm not an attorney, a CPA, a network engineer, or a marketer. So I hire those people to lend me their expertise and I do what they say, provided it makes sense. While you do need to know enough to evaluate whether someone is leading you the right way, you have to have a great team of experts.

You will never build a successful dental business if you DIY everything, especially when it comes to legal counsel and accounting. Don't be penny wise and pound foolish; hire a lawyer and an accountant who both really know the dental business and then listen.

Don't hire just anyone, either. Like dentists, financial professionals and lawyers have many subspecialties. In the financial world alone, you have tax accountants and controllers, CFOs and bookkeepers, and they all have their roles—you don't want to pay them to learn on the job. Hire competent, experienced people who can instantly help you get to your next steps.

» ***Don't trust the people you hire right away.*** You want to believe that you can trust everybody you hire, but I've gotten burned too many times, and watched colleagues get burned, to think that's true. For example, in 2017, the lady who had been my controller stole all of my data. She always kept her office door closed, and every time I walked in, she had a jump drive plugged into her computer. I never said anything, but I should have known something was up. I terminated her later that year, but she took the jump drive, stole my data, and then erased my database. I had to bring in an IT expert at $500 a day to recover as much of the data as possible. That hurt.

The moral: It doesn't hurt to be a *little bit* paranoid. By that I mean hire good people but vet them and watch them. Don't put them in a position to steal from you or abuse their power, and don't trust them blindly until they've earned that trust. Most of all, if something seems fishy about their results, investigate and then fire them if you don't like what you find. One bad apple can sabotage an entire company; I've seen it happen. Most of you have some embezzlement going on unless you've taken drastic steps to prevent it. Trust me, I know this from building twenty-five offices over the years. If it can happen, it will. It may be your cousin, but she will steal if you tempt her with poor money policies.

KEEP IN MIND

- **You can't run your business like a single-office practice.**
- **Profits matter more than revenue.**
- **Good associates don't matter if you can't keep them.**
- **Marketing is your lifeblood.**

What If You're Not Making Money?

My personal dentist is a Russian lady with an office near where I live in Los Angeles. I go to her because she's got a great touch. She doesn't speak a lot of English, but she's got great hands and even does cleanings herself. But she's old school; she doesn't even have a computer in her office. I've talked to her a little about my entrepreneurial ideas, but she's not interested. She's happy with her single office, doing things her way and earning a nice income. I think that's great.

Most dentists who know one end of a drill from the other can make a good living with a single office. If you're happy with that, terrific. But if you were happy with that, you wouldn't be reading this book. You probably want multiple offices, a consistent flow of profits, and some wealth. If you're not seeing those results, despite working endless hours and spending money on advertising, you're frustrated.

What are you doing wrong? There are some mistakes that I see pretty consistently:

1. ***Running more than two offices but still managing things like you have one.*** Most dentists struggle once they get past two locations. It's fairly easy to manage one location, because you're right there to see and communicate with everyone all day, every day. You can even do well if you have two offices and an associate or two, if you jump back and forth between offices. You don't have a system in place yet and you are still making lots of money. But here's where you spread yourself too thin: putting in two days at the central office, two days at the north office, and two days at the south office. Sound familiar?

   A great system will help you by giving everyone a template for every activity. Standard operating procedures, or SOPs, are a form of "this is how we do things here" documentation. As Michael Gerber writes, "Systems work so you don't have to."[8] You have to learn to work harder *on* your business than *in* your business.

Gerber also encourages us to think in terms of a business franchise format (BFF)—to build a dental business as though we plan to build 100 more exactly like it.[9] What would it look like? Operate like? Start there and try new iterations until you have the ideal model that works for your vision.

"Dentists have to figure out how to get away from chairside and work on scaling the business," says Darin Acopan, Vice President of Business Development for the DEO. "If you want to stay chairside, then you need to look at hiring a CEO. But after three locations, dentists will hit a wall. At that point, you need to look at bringing in an executive, because your staff at your offices doesn't know how to manage a larger practice."[10]

Alternatively, you could design your own self-development curriculum to help you become that trained dental CEO. Every entrepreneurial dentist should develop their own plan, even if you purchase a franchise concept, because your goals will differ from mine. Your business will only grow as much as your knowledge and judgment as an entrepreneur grow.

2. ***Not hiring someone to manage the day-to-day details of your offices or putting a replicable system in place.*** If you're trying to be a clinician, an office manager, and a visionary entrepreneur all at the same time, all you've done is create a tiring job for yourself. You can't think proactively; you just react. Without a system with rules and set

---

8 M. E. Gerber, *The E-Myth: Why Most Small Businesses Don't Work and What to Do about It* (New York: HarperBusiness, 1995).

9 M. E. Gerber, *The E-Myth*

10 Telephone interview, September 1, 2018.

procedures, things fall through the cracks. Tax errors, bad hires—costly mistakes can pile up.

You need a great operations manager once you get past two offices, period. I was fortunate to have a few good ones. My top operations manager was with me for many years. As a Registered Dental Assistant (RDA) and wife of a dentist, with a background in bookkeeping, she was very well qualified, and she loved to attend seminars to stay up on compliance issues, management software, billing, and more. You've got to have someone willing to work and grow, and you have to compensate them well, because the competition is waiting to steal the good ones away.

3. ***Having an eye on revenue coming in, but not on profit.*** This kills more small practices than anything else. If you're busy and bringing in a lot of money, but always seem to be break-even, you may not be paying attention to small costs that can add up quickly. I'm talking about advertising that's not working, overpriced supplies, giving raises to staff based on the calendar instead of merit, lab fees, overpaying associates—things like that.

If you don't have a head for finances, that's fine; make friends with a great dental CPA and have them scrutinize every area of expense with Scrooge-like skepticism. I found that working with an expert dental CFO who specialized in exit accounting and preparing you to go to market was money well spent. I would have consulted him earlier for guidance if I had known the benefits.

TALK TO THE EXPERT 

As a twenty-year veteran of Henry Schein's DSO division, it would be disingenuous of me not to emphasize the importance of picking the right distribution partner. Many of my young customers and colleagues don't recall a time when DSO juggernauts like Smile Brands, Pacific Dental, and Heartland were emerging. These giants faced growth challenges similar to what emerging groups do today.

The term "distributor partner" refers specifically to a distributor whose mission and culture is to embrace and understand the shifting marketplace in order to navigate it with you—not a distributor that is a supplier of "things." Strong distribution partners have the vision and industry position to explore and understand the marketplace from all angles, such as the changing economic and practice paradigms that are driving group practice growth. That includes appreciating the common challenges and pitfalls fledgling groups face, as well as cultivating solutions through industry innovators with best practices worth sharing and emulating.

—Kathleen Titus, Director of DSO/Group Practice, Henry Schein[11]

Invest in Your Future

If you make good choices and avoid making some egregious mistakes, the first thing you'll find is that it's nearly impossible for your one- or two-office

11 Email interview, November 17, 2018.

practice to fail. Dentistry is just that stable. The second thing you'll find is that you'll be well positioned to grow.

However, if expansion and wealth building are your long-term goals, you'll have to keep making good choices. The next time you talk with your banker, whether you're about to get a loan to open your first office or already have three, let him know the scope of your plans. Let him know that your ambition is to open one new location every year and to have 100 people working for you in five years. That will change the advice he gives you, but will also create the expectation that you'll be looking for bigger loans in the future.

Next, choose your niche carefully. I'll go into this in depth in Chapter 2, but I can say right now that selecting the right niche is probably the most important choice you'll make. It will determine everything else you do: your marketing, services, hiring, how you get paid—all of it.

Also, become a marketer. I came from a sales and marketing background and I love it. I love convincing people to do something that I think is in their best interest, even though they didn't know it until they met me. Some people think marketing is unseemly or dirty, but it's just letting people know a service is available and getting them to give you a chance.

There is a saying: "A person can die of thirst in the midst of water, if they don't ask for it." First, deliver a great service; then, *ask for the referral.* Ask for the positive review. Today, you're working for five-star ratings or reviews online. Everyone makes their buying decisions based on online reviews, and the great reviews don't happen by accident. They require marketing.

Take marketing courses, read everything you can get your hands on, and learn from successful dental marketing and branding campaigns. Why did they work so well? Was it because the dentists really knew their niche? Did they hire a terrific marketing agency? Was the messaging dead-on, or did the business buy just the right Google AdWords? Marketing is your lifeblood: It's what keeps new patients coming through your door.

Educate yourself. Write a blog, post regularly to Facebook, and learn to use all social media platforms—or hire someone. Remember, it's too expensive to have someone learn on the job. They need to come to you already an expert in online advertising and social media, or you have to find someone else.

One lesson I learned the hard way—hire cautiously and take care of your good associates . . . *within reason*. I lost a lot of good associate dentists a few years ago because the guy down the street was willing to pay them five or ten percent more than I was. You can do that, but if you overpay, you'll ruin your margins. The dentist who poached my people had fixed costs similar to mine, but he cut his margins in half by overpaying his associates.

Later on, he called and asked me to take my ex-employees back, which took a lot of nerve. I said, "Doc, you stole my people, and now you're running yourself out of business and want me to take them back?" He did $10 million that year, but his costs were $9.6 million, and a margin of 4 percent won't interest any buyer. He was looking at his revenues, but when the time comes to sell, buyers will be looking at your *profits*. Remember, it's what you keep, not what you earn.

Finally, invest time in learning how to think and act like a leader. Your days of managing every facet of your professional life are either over or will be over in the near future. Set aside one hour to make plans that will get you to your goal. What will you do today, tomorrow, this week? If you have twenty things a day on your to-do list and only get to five of them, that's still twenty-five important things you've done this week. That will put you far ahead of your competitors, who aren't really competing because they don't even realize they're in the game.

EYEING THE EXIT

This is a long game. The end could be twenty years or more away (it goes by quickly). All the more reason to up your game now. If you came up with your revenue goals after reading the introduction, start figuring out how many offices and patients you'll need to generate that revenue.

» How many locations will you need to open?
» How many patients will need to pass through your doors each year?
» How much revenue will each patient need to generate in a year?
» Can you get to that number offering the services you're offering, or do you need to make a change?
» What can you afford to pay associates and staff?
» What margins can you maintain?

Don't make yourself crazy trying to come up with all those answers on your own. If you don't have a good accountant, put this book down and hire one today. If you already have one, call him or her and work out these numbers. Trust me, they'll be very eye-opening and motivating.

CHAPTER 2

Your Niche Can Make You Rich

CHECK YOUR GPS

Hopefully, you have a clearer sense of where you want to go, so let's check in at this early stage.

- **Deliberately define your destination**: Based on what you've learned, what kind of business should you be building? What size?
- **Lock it into your internal GPS**: How many locations could you open in the next five years and how many people could you hire? Where would you find good associate dentists in your area, or ones you could convince to relocate from other areas?
- **Choose an ETA**: What funding options do you have for building out these locations and how long would it take for you to get the funds?
- **Devise your plan**: Is there a dental specialty that interests you, that you think you would find enjoyable, and that is relatively rare in your market? How would you launch yourself as a specialist in that area?
- **Get started now**: Start talking to banks and other potential

continued

sources of funding. Get proposals and, with your accountant, compare the upside and downside of each.

» **Trust the plan and keep moving.**

When I came to California, I was already planning to own the kind of business I had always wanted. But first, I worked as an associate for a couple of dentists who had big offices, and I noticed something interesting. No matter what office I went to for the dentist I worked for, if they found out that I was good with kids, they kept me busy all the time. The demand was outrageous. I became a sort of freelancer, going from one office to the next, and every office would book lots of kids for whenever I was going to be there. I became an in-demand freelance GP kids' dentist. The demographic was rich with opportunity for me.

The other thing I noticed was that while I liked the idea of owning multiple offices and having lots of dentists working for me, most of the dentists I worked for had never taken a business class. They had gotten where they were based mostly on luck and incompetent competitors. Not long after that, I decided that pediatric dental care would be my niche, and in January 1994, I opened my first Kids Dental Kare location.

At least, I tried. As luck would have it, the 6.7 Northridge earthquake hit just in time to destroy some of our building renovations. The California Dental Association gave me $2,000 to help repair some of the damage, and on February 15, 1994, I opened the doors of my first California pediatric dental office.

But I wasn't satisfied with just being a kids' dentist. There were lots of those. While I visited local schools and other general dental practices, educating people about my services and letting parents know I was in the community and open for business, I also became aware of another way I could target consumers with even greater precision.

Most people know that Los Angeles has a large Latino population, but I realized that my practice was actually located within a part of the city that had a high concentration of Armenians. In fact, in 2000, that stretch of East Hollywood bisected by Sunset Boulevard would be named "Little Armenia."

That was my first target audience. It wouldn't be the only population I served, but I was fairly sure that few dentists—and even fewer pediatric dentists—were targeting the city's Armenian community. According to the 1990 census, there were about 115,000 Armenians living in Greater Los Angeles, which was more than enough of a patient pool for me to build a thriving business. Now I had to refine my marketing to appeal to the Armenians living in the immediate geographic area.

I hired a company to create cable TV commercials—in Russian, which many Armenians speak. That was a big, expensive risk for a new practice, but I really wanted to put distance between me and my nearest competitors, and the strategy worked. Armenian parents loved that I was speaking to them in their language, and they soon brought their children to me in droves.

I began advertising my practice on neighborhood billboards, in print ads, on bus benches, and virtually anywhere that parents might see my message. Often, those ads were in Russian, too, and the burning of lots of ad dollars brought me a growing, loyal patient base. But I knew I was really established when some of my competitors began to send people to spy on my practice to learn how I was growing so quickly. Some competitors even planted staff in my office with orders to download client lists, photograph my offices, and take screenshots of our computerized appointment schedules.

The cutthroat competition was proof that I'd targeted the right niche. I'd made it.

THINK

- **» The benefits of specializing in a niche.**
- **» Specializing makes people perceive you as an expert.**
- **» Niche marketing is an elite business skill.**

Having a Niche Lets You Build Your Skills

If you told me I could only choose one strategy for creating a multi-location, wealth-building dental business, it would be specializing in serving the right niche. There are many reasons for this that I'll get into, but one of the most basic is that having a niche focuses your efforts, energy, time, and resources in a way that being a generalist doesn't.

Early in your career, especially if you're only running one office, your fortunes will depend largely on how people perceive you as a dentist. Patients and the general public will judge you to a lesser degree based on your marketing, your staff, and your facility, but word will spread based on your technical prowess. Until you're able to hire associates, the number of patients you can see—and the amount of money you can make—will depend on how quickly you can deliver quality dental care. So it stands to reason that if you're a general dentist who's doing cosmetics, oral surgery, crown and bridge, and a dozen other services, there won't be enough hours in the day for you to develop more-than-average skill and speed at all of them.

When I first came to California, I worked for a dentist I'll call Dr. B., who had a practice in the city of Cerritos. He amazed me, because he could place stainless steel crowns (SSC) faster than anyone I had ever seen. I had been placing crowns for a few years and thought I was pretty good, but he was incredible. Finally I said, "Doctor, how did you get to be so quick and so good at doing crowns?"

He replied, "Lanier, you get your first 10,000 in and you'll be quick, too." (This was before *Outliers* by Malcolm Gladwell came out.) I have found this to be true over and over again: *You can't become an expert overnight.* You can learn a lot from others' experiences, but sooner or later, you have to get in the water and swim. If practice makes perfect, then doing something five days a week for ten years will make you one of the best in the world. You'll be fast, turn patients over more quickly, give them great outcomes that will make them want to tell their friends about you, and increase your income.

The same applies to business skills. You have to start now if you are going to get your 10,000 hours in to reach expert businessperson status.[12]

Specialization or Segmentation Earns You Referrals

Having a niche forces you to focus. It impacts how you work—but also how you train, the equipment you buy, the look and feel of your offices, and, certainly, your marketing. And it has a gigantic impact on how people perceive you, which can give a serious boost to your earning power. According to PayScale.com, these are the median annual 2019 salaries of various dental specialties:

- General dentist: $125,977
- Orthodontist: $172,504

---

12 Malcolm Gladwell, *Outliers: The Story of Success* (New York: Little, Brown and Co., 2008).

» Pediatric dentist: $174,306
» Periodontist: $176,921
» Endodontist: $202,948
» Oral surgeon: $220,159[13]

Based on those numbers, by choosing to limit my practice to pediatrics instead of being a generalist, I gave myself a big raise. It can also be a lot easier to grow your practice as a specialist, because you're not trying to compete with every other dentist out there. I was seeing a lot of Medicaid kids, whom a lot of specialists didn't want to treat—and most GPs couldn't treat—so I was generating referrals like crazy. I hired more GPs and pediatric dentists, as well as an orthodontist, and started making money.

Having a niche also increases people's confidence in you. When you limit your practice, they assume you've had special training in that area and are more competent than the generalist. It might not be true, but that perception will get you more direct business and more referrals, because your fellow dentists will have more confidence in you, too.

Referrals are a huge part of any dentist's business development, and that's great because referrals are personal and geography-specific. Another dentist will only refer a patient to you if he's confident in your technical skill and the patient doesn't have to drive too far to get to your office. Patients have to really feel confident in you—and love your personality and that of your staff—before they will recommend you to a friend or write a five-star review online. You have to work for referrals.

That's where the repetitive work as a specialist (limited practice) is valuable. The more the word gets out that you're highly skilled at veneers, endodontics, or orthodontics, the more referrals you'll get. No dentist with

13 www.payscale.com

any sense will refer a patient to someone whose skills he's not 100 percent confident in, because nothing wrecks a patient relationship faster than a referral dentist who screws up the job. It's terribly embarrassing. Likewise, you can work to refer patients you don't see to a dentist that will cross-refer with you.

To be fair, being a specialist or focusing your practice can feel limiting, and it's not for everyone. There's a saying: "A specialist is a person who knows more and more about less and less." If you're an entrepreneurial thinker, it can be smart to specialize, but it's not a deal breaker if you don't. You can easily brand yourself as a generalist who mostly does one or two procedures. But as you build your practice and hire associates, hire some who are specialists in high-cost, high-value procedures. That will set you apart and gain you referrals, even if you're a general dentist, yourself.

LUCRATIVE LARRY'S ADVICE ON . . . CHOOSING A NICHE

One of the basic rules of being an entrepreneur is "Find an unmet need and meet it." What groups with money and a need for dentistry in your region aren't being served? Do people in your area who want to see a specialist, such as a cosmetic dentist, face a long drive? Those are "seams," weaknesses that you can turn into your niche.

Specializing by Patient Group

If you look back at that list of specialties and their salaries, you might notice something interesting. Go back and have a quick look at it again.

Did you notice the break in the pattern? No? That's okay. Out of all those specialties, pediatric dentistry is the only one based on serving a specific patient group, not a specific type of procedure, such as oral surgery or fitting braces. That highlights an important point:

You can also specialize by serving a specific type of patient.

If you like being a generalist but still want to specialize because you appreciate how beneficial it can be for your brand and business, just choose a type of patient that you like working with. You can also choose a patient group that's affluent, has a big population near you, or is underserved by other dentists. Here are some examples of what I mean:

» Seniors
» Millennials
» Women
» The wealthy
» LGBTQ
» People who hate the dentist
» Medicaid patients
» An ethnic or religious group
» Busy executives
» People who live in a certain city or region

For the most part, those people won't need dental services that are very different from what any other patient would need. But if they feel like you understand their needs or provide services that others can't (for example, fast lunchtime cleanings for on-the-go businesspeople), you'll earn their patronage.

Prestige Doesn't Matter; Profit Does

If you do choose to limit your niche, you'll have a big edge over a lot of your competitors, because they just won't do it. I never understood it. I got a lot of raised eyebrows from other dentists when they found out that most of my business came from low-income families whose kids were on Medicaid. My background, as you may remember, was as a public health dentist. I had determined, before I completed my four-year obligation with the New Orleans clinic, that I would find a way to address the severe access problems faced by the poor and underserved.

When I left New Orleans in 1987 to come to Los Angeles, I tried to learn as much as I could. I took a lot of classes in orthodontics and cosmetic dentistry, and I became fairly good at cosmetics. But it wasn't something in high demand like pediatrics. Almost every dentist I knew became a cosmetic dentist to some degree. I liked working with kids, but that wasn't in the "glamour lane" of dentistry.

Everyone I talked to wanted to be doing what was flashy, to be able to brag that they "sold a crown for $1,500!" This is highly specialized work and many dentists build lucrative practices selling high-ticket procedures, but don't think that you're the only one who can perform these procedures. To make money and become an Entrepreneur Dentist without having to do it all yourself, you're going to have to be able to recruit other dentists and leverage their time. You have to find a way to share work with others so you can grow the business.

Most dentists don't understand a thing about business and don't care to. They don't mind being employees forever. They can become highly paid technicians earning big salaries as hired guns for other dentists. But they are always going to be trading their time for money, and you'll never get rich doing that. If you do what I'm teaching you, which is to build a platform that makes money for you when you're not working—the definition of an investor—you *will* get rich.

Niche Marketing Makes Dentists Nervous

That's the path I intended to follow, so as soon as I could, I launched Kids Dental Kare. I crowdsourced the name and the logo among the girls at the practice I was working at, being careful not to let the owners know I was planning to compete with them. Limiting myself to pediatrics was an easy decision for me; it was what I knew. However, this limiting strategy is not for most dentists—or for most entrepreneurs in any field. We want to try to be all things to all people. Turning away any business makes entrepreneurs *very* nervous, even though it's the best way to grow your business.

In business, your natural impulse is to try to grab any and all business you can get, especially in the beginning when money is tight. But while most of the dentists I saw didn't know business theory from a hole in the ground, the ones who did were specialists. Niche marketing is an elite business skill, because you're only going after customers who will give you the biggest ROI.

Think about it this way: If I'm a general dentist and I run a quarter-page advertisement every Monday in the metro section of the *Los Angeles Times*, it's going to cost me about $5,000 a week. I'll reach about a million people, but I'll be lucky to get ten new patients. That's a terrible ROI. Why so poor? Because I'm just another dentist. There's no reason for someone to call me over anyone else with a DDS after his name.

Instead, let's say I decide to specialize in busy executives. I run ads in three business-oriented publications, including the *Los Angeles Business Journal*, for about half the cost of my *Times* ad. My niche tells the reader, "I understand you, the busy professional who doesn't have much time for oral care," and I get about forty new patients in the same amount of time. My ROI is sky-high. I'm excluding ninety-five percent of my potential market, but so what? I have a big chunk of a demographic that needs what I'm offering and has the means to pay a premium price.

That's the value of choosing a niche. You don't have to be all things to all people. You just need to be of value to a group that needs what you're offering and sends you new patients.

DO

- **Choose your niche.**
- **If you're going to take classes, make them business classes.**
- **Pick something you're good at but enjoy.**
- **Figure out how to "own" your niche.**

How to Choose Your Niche

But what niche to choose? That's the critical decision. What criteria do you even start with in choosing? First of all, let me be clear on something: Serving a niche does not mean you have to be a technical specialist, such as an oral surgeon. You can be a general dentist who only does fillings, extractions, implants—whatever. You don't necessarily have to take more classes and invest time and money in specialized training (though you certainly can if you want to polish your skills). If you do decide to take personal development classes, make most of them classes in business and marketing. Learn how supply chains work. Learn something about HR. Learn how ad buys are priced and how email marketing campaigns work.

There are three main ways you can specialize:

1. The services you provide (extractions, cosmetics, implants, etc.)

2. The patients you serve (kids, seniors, women, high-income, middle-income, people on Medicaid)
3. The geographic area you serve

When you define yourself as serving a specific market or providing a specific service, that's called *positioning*. Your goal should be to position yourself in a way that—

- Gives you access to a patient base large enough to provide you with a steady flow of business and referrals, with the means to pay you (cash or insurance);
- Sets you apart from other dentists in your geographic area; and
- Creates the impression that you're delivering exceptional value that other dentists aren't. Your caring attitude and that of your staff can be a differentiator. Your office hours can be the convenience factor that makes a difference. But if you do what everyone else is doing, why should you expect different results?

That's how you not only grow your practice but also fend off rivals who try to steal your patients, staff, and associates. If you're known as "the" dentist who takes amazing care of seniors in your area, or who closes out of respect for the Islamic high holy days, your competitors will have a harder time taking you down.

In general, when you're looking for a niche, ask the following questions:

1. Is this niche large enough or affluent enough to provide me with a level of profit that fits my goals?
2. How many patients could I realistically expect to get from this niche per month, and how much could I expect to earn per patient?

3. Is this niche already saturated with dentists positioned like me, or is there room for someone who cares for the people I'm targeting or provides the services I specialize in?
4. Is this niche likely to provide me with a strong referral base?
5. Will I enjoy working in this niche (i.e., do I like working with kids, or do I like doing fillings and extractions eighty percent of the time)?
6. Are there any language barriers or cultural and religious concerns that would prevent me from connecting with this niche or make it hard for the people in it to trust me?
7. What will it cost me to shift my practice and marketing to target this niche, and is that number acceptable?

If the answers look good, and the numbers work with your annual income and profit goals, then you might have your niche. But there's more to choosing a niche than purely empirical information. You should also give strong consideration to what you feel comfortable doing, what you like doing, and what you're really good at. Avoid procedures or groups of people that you don't like.

This works even if you're still serving as an associate for another dentist. Tell your employer, "This is what I'm really good at, and I could do a lot of this and be a benefit to you, but if you're putting me on this other thing, I'm not going to be very good at it." That's better for you, and better for your employer, because people always show up with more enthusiasm and do a better job when they enjoy what they're doing.

Be Profit-Minded but Don't Forget

Even if you like something or are proficient at it, it still might not be your niche. If you're running a single office and trying to specialize, you have to balance what you enjoy and what you're good at with what can turn a profit. Profit has to come first, because your goal isn't to run a nonprofit but to exit rich.

One example I've experienced is kids with severe disabilities. I rarely worked on them at Kids Dental Kare because they have unique needs and take up a lot of time. Even if it took me twice as long to take care of them as a non-disabled patient, insurance still paid me the same amount. There was no way I could make a profit on them. That's where you'll find tension between your empathy for patients and your profit motive. Yes, you need to make money, but you're also caring for human beings. Find the balance between the two that works for you, as I did.

My balance was that I treated some kids with disabilities anyway as my way of giving back to the community that supported me, and to help these kids that would get lost in the cracks otherwise. Such patients won't directly benefit your bottom line, but they will be vitamin shots for your public image and your satisfaction with your work. When you do work like that, patients will love you so much that they will go out of their way to refer others. You may have lost money initially, but the work will pay such great dividends that you'll do well by doing good.

This also applies to the twelve- or thirteen-year-old with supra-gingival calculus on a few teeth, where the young doctor comes all the way to the front office to find out if they are going to be paid for removing it. Almost any insurance company (as well as Medicaid) considers supra-gingival calculus to be part of the prophy. There are doctors who don't want to remove calculus because they are only getting paid for a prophy. This shows a lack of understanding. If there is an ultrasonic scaler chairside, it would take less time to remove the calculus than it takes to walk to the front to ask about it. This is also a great opportunity to show the parent and child what and where the calculus is and how you're going to remove it with no extra charge. Marketing, my friends . . . at *every* opportunity.

This is something that requires a big-picture thinker. Most people are looking for instant gratification; they don't want to do any pro bono work and wait for ROI down the line. Dentists are no different. Most Entrepreneur Dentists aren't doing pro bono work, so they get judged unfairly by people who say, "You're looking too hard at profit." Yes, that's what I'm supposed to be doing! There's no one who stays in business who's not looking hard at expenses, margins, and profits all the time and making some ruthless decisions.

But if you're forced to choose, try to do what you love. When you love your work, you'll find a way to be successful at it. Also, in the end, what we do is just as much about taking care of people as it is about making money. "Self as servant" is the ideal mental state to be in. If you can see yourself as a servant regardless of what you're doing, it changes your attitude immediately. You may be a very well-paid servant, but you're still a servant, because your livelihood depends on your ability to serve others.

I had a father who brought his disabled daughter to me for years, and every time I finished working on her teeth, he would give me a hug and thank me. She was this adorable little thing in a wheelchair who couldn't even brush her own teeth, and caring for her was about more than money. It was about feeling good about what I did. That's part of our compensation, too.

Watch profits, but never forget that you're helping people. The moment you take your eye off that ball, you're in trouble. I've seen practices where the dentist is all about the money and not really thinking about the care or services, and that's not a viable model. You're dealing with human beings who trust you, and multiply that by ten when you're working with children.

You've got to deliver genuine, compassionate, expert care. Another pearl I stole from Zig Ziglar was "Nobody cares how much you know until they know how much you care."[14]

I once terminated an associate who had great technical skill but a very poor chairside manner. He was driving patients away with his poor attitude. It reflected badly upon everyone. He thought his production should be the only thing that mattered. He was wrong.

Here's where some Entrepreneur Dentists hit the danger zone. This can be a profitable profession, and if they start making a lot of money really fast, the money becomes the point. They start to believe their own hype, think they have the Midas touch, and stop watching what's going on behind the scenes. But no one will ever care about your business like you do, and no one will ever run it the way you would. So they take their eyes off the road, and the next thing you know, the business is in the ditch. My advice is always "inspect what you expect."

This is about finding a balance between specialization/niche segmentation, profitability, sustainability, and delivering value for the patient. You have to find that sweet spot. If you do, you'll do well.

TALK TO THE EXPERT

I own a consulting company called Doctors Making Money, and for the past fifteen years, I've worked in a variety of marketing niches and have been under Dr. Lanier's mentorship. In that time, one of the most important realizations I've made is that doctors tend to underestimate the importance of great marketing. Sure, they may have a marketing budget or a strategy,

14 Zig Ziglar, *Better Than Good: Creating a Life You Can't Wait to Live* (New York: Integrity Publishers, 2006).

but that does not translate into great marketing. However, before we get into *great* marketing, let's begin by simply defining "marketing" itself.

Marketing is the process of communicating what you have to offer for your patients. Marketing *is not* advertising. Marketing is a strategy, while advertising is one of the many actions you can take within marketing. Know the difference so that you don't commit the common mistake of interchanging the two and putting all your eggs in one marketing basket.

Another thing I've learned, especially while working with Dr. Lanier and Kids Dental Kare, is that marketing is not a one-size-fits-all strategy. The opposite is true. The market and patients are constantly changing. New platforms come along and old ones become obsolete. Therefore, having a clown outside your practice may have attracted new patients ten years ago, while now, a well-placed Facebook ad may get the same, if not better, results. The key is to stay open-minded to these changes, and know when to make a shift in your marketing strategy.

Television ads were a huge deal for Kids Dental Kare many years ago, but Dr. Lanier recognized that the cost of such commercials started to not give him the ROI he wanted. He shifted his strategy to more robust and cost-efficient online marketing. However, he didn't abandon older tactics, such as calendars or school presentations. He simply added another marketing layer to support his current efforts, while eliminating activities that simply didn't make financial sense anymore. Businesses that fail to shift with the times and evolve their marketing to fit current patients' needs are doomed to fail.

—Keu Reyes, Marketing Consultant,
Doctors Making Money[15]

15 Email interview, November 28, 2018.

Know Your Niche

Once you have a niche in mind, before you commit, do your research. That's not an issue if you're building a niche around a dental specialty, but it could be if you're planning to specialize in a geographic area—and it definitely will be important if you're going to specialize in a specific demographic. What's the demand? How profitable is the niche? Can you dominate this area?

If you're going to position yourself as serving a particular area, learn about the lifestyle in that area. For example, if the area is densely urban with bad traffic, the people who live there probably walk or bike everywhere. So you'll probably want to choose an office location that's near a streetcar or light-rail line, and you'll want to have bike racks outside your front door.

This becomes critical when you're thinking about serving an ethnic or religious community, or a group like seniors or the LGBTQ community. Are there cultural barriers that you're not aware of? For instance, Asians generally like to see Asian dentists. If you're not Asian, but you burn a lot of capital building an office in an Asian neighborhood and targeting Asians with your marketing, you're probably going to waste a lot of money, unless you hire Asian dentists and staff. Know your market well before you launch.

There's plenty of research out there in professional periodicals, such as *Dental Economics*. According to that publication, twenty-three percent of Americans are afraid of going to the dentist, a fear called *odontophobia*. What's really eye-opening is that women over age forty are more likely to have anxiety about seeing the dentist than any other group.[16] If you're planning on serving a niche built around middle-aged women, you'd better know that and design your business around allaying those fears, or you'll go bankrupt!

When you're considering a niche, learn all you can about it. Read academic

---

16 Vicki McManus Peterson, "Reaching the Right Patients: People Who Fear the Dentist," *Dental Economics*, August 1, 2018, www.dentaleconomics.com/articles/print/volume-108/issue-8/practice/reaching-the-right-patients-people-who-fear-the-dentist.html.

journals and dentistry trade magazines, but also talk to people from the group you want to serve. Ask them about attitudes toward dentists, oral care, and payment. Ask about dietary practices that could affect oral health or create challenges for you. Ask about religious or gender practices that could limit your opportunities. For example, conservative Muslim men may be unwilling to send their wives or daughters to a male dentist. If you're a man and want to start an office in a largely Muslim neighborhood, you'd better have some female associates and hygienists working for you.

It pays to learn about—

» The availability of insurance;
» The group's willingness to see dentists who don't share their ethnic or religious heritage;
» Practices related to cleanliness, TVs in the treatment room, and so on;
» How often a particular group historically goes to the dentist; and
» How much of the population typically speaks English.

This last detail helped me when I decided to target the Armenians in my part of Los Angeles. I knew many of them spoke Russian and I assumed that they were used to seeing advertisements that were mostly in English and Spanish, so I made a bet that they would be delighted at seeing ads in their language—and I won that bet. That happened because I took the time to learn about that niche.

By the way, you can have more than one niche. If you have multiple offices in multiple locations in a diverse urban area, you could be the dentist for the African-American community in one neighborhood, the dentist for recent immigrants in another neighborhood, and the dentist for the kids of wealthy divorced moms in a third neighborhood. Just make sure you keep your marketing—and your office décor—separate and straight.

You can also combine niches. You could position yourself as a dentist who just does fillings and extractions for kids, or who just does veneers for women. Find the needs that aren't being met or a community that's not being served and make them yours.

Remember—in choosing a niche, always be thinking about profit. What could you do that will have the highest profit margin? Then you have to commit. You have to be ready to say, "I'm going to limit my practice to these high-margin services. All of these other services that I don't enjoy, that eat up time and bring me less money, I'm going to refer out." I did that for years and never had anybody look at me crosswise. Choose what will be profitable and then stick with it.

KEEP IN MIND

- **"Owning" a niche is about psychology.**
- **Say *no* more often than you say *yes*.**
- **Be relentless.**

Own Your Niche

Once you're in a niche, the challenge becomes staying there. Usually, that's not because you're *not* making money but, rather, because you see other niches and are tempted to try them out. You're like a recently married man who sees a beautiful woman walk by and thinks, "I'm not going to be with the same woman for the rest of my life, am I?" Resist that temptation and stay in your lane.

The reason is simple: The better and more comfortable you get at the kind of dentistry you're practicing, the faster and more efficiently you'll be able to serve patients, the more money you'll make, and the sooner you'll be able to expand.

Here's an example of being uncomfortable. After college, when I was working for the U.S. Public Health Service, I saw some adults who needed oral surgery—who were in so much pain that they were crying. We didn't have an oral surgeon, so I started doing the surgery. I had an oral surgery book with diagrams of everything, and I would get the patient's X-rays, go through the book, and find the images that matched my X-ray. Then I'd do the surgery. If I got stuck in the middle of the procedure, I'd stop and say, "Excuse me. Let me grab something here," and leave, with the patient still sitting there with my assistant. I'd turn the book to page 187, find what I needed, and go back to work.

I became quite competent at surgical extractions while I worked there, which let me help a lot of people. But I am an Entrepreneur Dentist and I have to weigh risks and see the big picture. When I started my private practice, my friends convinced me that the risk/reward ratio was too weighted against me to continue doing that kind of work—even though I enjoyed doing it.

They were right to warn me. There is a lot of risk out there and you have a lot of years to use your dental license, so for God's sake, don't ever do anything to jeopardize that license or your ability to practice. That license is a license to print money, but you have to protect it like the goose that lays the golden egg.

Contrast that with my first practice, where I got really comfortable and fast working on kids. With the repetition and the predictability, my office became a well-oiled machine. Denise and Sharon, the first two dental assistants I had (and whom I will remember forever), could hand me an X-ray while I was walking down a hallway and, because I had done so many extractions, I could tell them what to set up with one look, without ever breaking stride. They knew what I needed before I did, because they knew me as well. We were fast, and that meant we were profitable.

That's what having a niche can do. Having the right niche elevates you from a practice to a *business*. To really make money, you want to be doing what you like and what you're comfortable doing as often as possible. Once you get to the point where you can provide great outcomes without thinking about it, and you feel good about what you're doing, you can start thinking, "How do I monetize this?"

Once you're in a niche, your goal should be to "own" it—that is, to have anyone in the area or group you serve think of you first when they think about going to the dentist or giving a referral . . . and for other dentists who might want to horn in on your territory to think twice. You want to be the "Armenian dentist" or the "Christian dentist" or the "transgender-friendly dentist" or what have you.

Here are some of the keys if you want to own your niche:

» ***Say no more often than you say yes.*** I referred out millions of dollars in non-pediatric business in my career because I was determined to stay in my lane. When you stray from your niche, you dilute your brand. People stop thinking of you as "their" dentist, and that's dangerous. If you build your practice just for that thirty-eight-year-old female who drives a BMW, make her your avatar and you can make money from her. Eliminate everybody else who doesn't fit that profile. Refer everyone else out.

» ***Be careful about combining services that don't work well together.*** Orthodontics and pediatrics go together, but orthodontists are specialists, and they don't want me looking over their shoulder telling them what to do with my patients. I really don't like being responsible for specialist work that I can't monitor. Also, because orthodontics is a volume practice, when I booked orthodontists, I had to shut down my pediatric services for the day. I was robbing Peter to pay Paul and hurting my core business. I couldn't make money that way, so I rarely brought ortho into my offices.

» ***Curate your services.*** Unless you're a specialist in one type of dentistry, you might be tempted to be a jack-of-all-trades for your target patients. That's a mistake. Your time will be more manageable, and your business more profitable, if you limit yourself to a suite of high-demand services that you know you or your associate dentist can perform well and quickly.

For example, at Kids Dental Kare, I did just eight things, including exams and cleanings (I called it "exam-prophy"), extractions, silver fillings and crowns, white fillings and crowns, and space maintainers for after an extraction. That was it. A well-trained chimpanzee could have done them. But I did them well, and they were needed by every kid at one time or another.

» ***Have a consistent message.*** Have a message, a look, and a brand identity that never changes. People need to feel like they know you and that you're there to stay.

» ***Finally, be relentless.*** Owning a niche takes time and repetition. You need time for your marketing to penetrate the minds of the people you want as your patients, time for them to refer people they know, time for your reputation to build. Once you choose your niche, set up your marketing, put your head down, and do good work.

I've tried to teach my son the power of relentlessness. We often go walking in the hills above Los Angeles, up near Griffith Park. Eventually, he'll say, "Dad, can we just stop and turn around now? We've gone far enough." I'll reply, "You're going to the top, because when we left the house, we said we were going to the top." That's just as true in business. Keep going and don't worry about what other people do. Go until it's done.

EYEING THE EXIT 

To exit with millions of dollars, choose a niche that's sustainable. It's great to find a dental specialty that's in high demand, a population that's growing in wealth, or a neighborhood with a lot of young families. That's what makes rich dentists.

This is where it pays to think outside the box. For example, based on population changes, health trends, and demographics, these are some possible niches that might be worth exploring for the Entrepreneur Dentist:

- Home health care
- Nursing homes
- Skilled nursing centers
- Diabetes and cancer patients
- Millennials
- Freelance professionals and independent contractors
- The extremely affluent

Do your research, get the numbers, survey possible competitors, and see if there's a million-dollar niche with your name on it.

CHAPTER 3

Location, Location, Location

CHECK YOUR GPS

If you've chosen your niche, you're one step closer to your million-dollar business. Let's review how far you've come.

- **Deliberately define your destination**: Which niche (or niches) are you going to serve, and what are you going to do to own them and turn them into profit machines?
- **Lock it into your internal GPS**: How much does each patient from your niche need to generate per year for your long-term goal to be viable?
- **Choose an ETA**: If you're going to pursue other niches when you open other offices, which ones?
- **Devise your plan**: How will you customize your business to serve your niche? How will you change your marketing, physical location, décor, staff training, patient services, or associates to suit your niche?
- **Get started now**: Start researching other potentially profitable niches that you could go after by opening other locations in the future.
- **Trust the plan and keep moving.**

In their classic book *Positioning*, Al Ries and Jack Trout talk about trying to position yourself as number one or number two in some niche. No one seems to remember number three or four. When your brand owns the top of the market, you have established your position.[17] In this case, your location is the same as your position; and both, correctly handled, will place you right at the top of the consumer's mind.

With dental offices, the location should be based first on *demographics*. You want to fish where the fish are biting. Your survey should be so specific that you know exactly what zip code you want your office in based on the demographics alone. After that, it's a numbers game: You want brokers sending you listings for as many buildings as possible that fit your specifications. Location is the key to your success in so many ways that you'll want to spend a bit of time studying it before you commit to anything.

Know What Your Niche Needs

After my first year in business, my practice had grossed $1.1 million. I knew there was a lot more potential to be tapped, so I soon opened my second practice, positioning my office in a predominantly Latino area. I hired an experienced marketing professional, advertised on the local Spanish-speaking TV networks, and continued to work hard (but efficiently).

Soon, my practices were growing, and the money was rolling in. By my third year in business, I had also opened my third practice. My strategy was to stay within a set of concentric circles, targeting areas with a high concentration of children who needed specialized pediatric services. That made it clear to me that choosing the right location—a location that appeals to your

---

17 Al Ries and Jack Trout, *Positioning: The Battle for Your Mind* (New York: McGraw-Hill, 1986).

niche—is a critical, but underappreciated, part of success for an Entrepreneur Dentist.

Whatever you choose as your niche, it's a very, very good idea to open an office with that niche in mind. Dentistry is local; people will usually not stray too far from their home or office to get their teeth cleaned. So, apart from choosing the right niche for you, choosing the location of your office—and of each office after that—is critical.

I went for a specific demographic profile. Apart from the Armenians I marketed to in the beginning, my niche was low-income kids, mostly in Latino areas. Like I said earlier, they were covered by Medicaid, so their parents would take them for dental care even if they wouldn't get care themselves. But I knew that if I wanted to get those Latino parents in my door, I needed to be on a high-visibility corner and have a building with beautiful colors.

I knew that I needed a parking lot, because everyone in California drives. I needed to be on the first floor, because people with kids don't want to be going up elevators. Since California is mostly flat, I also wanted a building with a ramp that parents could roll a stroller up. My niche, and knowing what the people in my niche wanted, drove my decisions about real estate. My ideal office space was a former bank building. Banks usually have signalized corners with high traffic, good visibility, and good ingress and egress into and out of their parking lot. For some specialties that may not be necessary, especially if you get most of your patients from referrals like an endodontist would. If that's you, you may even prefer to be in a high-rise with plenty of other GPs and specialists. It all depends on—say it with me—your niche.

Location will determine a great deal about how profitable you can be as a dentist, and location is closely linked to your niche. Let's say you're a specialist doing $2,000 crowns for rich people in Bel Air. You're getting lots of referrals, and you need to treat each one like a king or queen. You can't locate your office in a sketchy strip mall along a frontage road; wealthy matrons in

BMWs will avoid you. You need a beautiful building in a prestigious part of town, with a lease to match. That's part of your cost of doing business. Alignment and congruence are necessary parts of the thinking that should guide your decisions.

There's a lot to think about when you're considering location, including whether you care about living close to your office. I have a friend who had a big pediatric practice located in South Gate, a lower-middle-class suburb southeast of Los Angeles. But he lived in Marina Del Rey, a wealthy coastal city about an hour away in L.A. traffic. He told me his friends used to ask him, "Why don't you have your practice here in Marina Del Rey?"

He replied, "If I did that, I'd probably have to live in South Gate." He knew that the cost of maintaining an office in Marina Del Rey would be so much higher than South Gate that it would ruin his margins. But there was another reason he wanted to stay in South Gate.

That's a poorer socioeconomic region, which, like it or not, generally means poorer oral hygiene and a need for more dental care around cavities and fillings—which also means more money for a dentist. He was doing very well in South Gate. Marina Del Rey is rich and mostly white, and there will be comparatively few cavities in a place like that. You might get orthodontic work, but the rest is likely to be cleanings. It's going to be harder to make money. If you're selling burglar alarms, you don't go to the rich, gated communities. You go to the poor neighborhoods, where there's a lot of crime. Dentists can follow the need, and that's what you should be doing.

The trouble is, too few dentists choose their locations based on what will be most profitable. They usually choose them based on what their peers will think. Who cares? That's like buying a budget-breaking Mercedes to impress the neighbors when a Corolla is within your budget and will get you to your destination just as quickly.

Dentistry is pretty democratic, unlike medicine. In medicine, it's all about who went to Harvard. In the dental world, it doesn't matter what school you graduated from or what you got on the National Boards. Status doesn't matter. What matters is having a sustainable patient base and a solid business model that you enjoy and that creates the greatest profit over the long term.

Nobody will give you the side-eye for being in this for the money. If you can build a high-value practice and sell it for millions, you'll have plenty of status.

- **Your offices need to be busy.**
- **You need a location that works for associate dentists.**
- **A busy practice is dummy-proof.**

This Isn't Vegas

In building a successful business that you can sell for life-changing money, it really is about location, location, location. Most people don't think about dental care the way they do about going to the doctor. For better or worse, going to the doctor is more of an event, more life-or-death in context, even if it's just for a routine physical. People are more willing to drive a longer distance or inconvenience themselves because the medical profession has greater prestige associated with it than dentistry—even though what we do is just as important for people's health.

For the approximately sixty-five percent of Americans who see a dentist regularly, dental care is less of an event and more a part of a regular routine.

That's good for you *if*—and it's an important if—you've made your offices convenient for your patients by locating them well and providing facilities tailored to your niche. If parents with small children can get them into your building with ease . . . if seniors using walkers can get through the doors without fear of falling . . . if busy professionals can find your office quickly in traffic because you have good signage and your address is clearly visible . . . you'll probably do well.

That's because making money as a dentist is about volume more than individual fees. That's why dentists who locate where they'll get heavy patient traffic are smarter than the ones who locate in wealthy areas with high rents. Think about it like going to Las Vegas. When most people come back from Vegas, they talk about that big slot machine payoff or the run of hands they had at the blackjack table. They don't talk about the fact that, overall, they lost $1,500 for the weekend.

Dentists do the same thing. I've known specialists who operated in Westwood (near UCLA) and Beverly Hills who would tell you about the afternoon they sold eight porcelain veneers for $15,000. That's great. But what about all the time that same week that they sat around watching CNN because so few patients actually came in to pay those high fees? They don't mention that part.

People in lower-volume, higher-income areas still deserve great dental care, of course. And some dentists who run practices in those areas still build multimillion-dollar businesses, to be sure. But when you locate in areas where the traffic is lower and the rents and overhead are much higher—not to mention what you have to pay your dental assistants and hygienists—you have a smaller margin of error. My offices were in lower-income areas, and they were always busy, from the time we opened the doors until the time we turned out the lights. That translates to a steady flow of revenue. But when you're dependent on affluent individuals and families to come in every six months for a cleaning, or once every two years for a big-ticket item like veneers, your revenue stream becomes very volatile, with high spikes but deep troughs.

So yes, when you're located in one of those markets, you get to brag about your big-ticket patients, but at the end of the month, how much money did you take home? It's like playing a lot of bad poker hands in the hopes of getting a royal flush. If you play long enough, you'll eventually get it, but how much will you lose in the meantime?

LUCRATIVE LARRY'S ADVICE ON . . . WORKING WITH A REAL ESTATE LAWYER

Don't be dumb. Lawyers are expensive, but when you're dealing with something like a lease that can lock you into a piece of real estate for ten years, the old saying applies: "You can pay me now, or you can pay me later." Consider the attorney's fee as an investment in building a business free of booby traps that will snap shut on you years down the line. Quit being cheap and spend what it takes to get good advice.

It's Not the Building; It's the Patients

A building isn't a business. That's the attitude I want you to have. A building is a place to serve patients, and it's patients that will get you paid. My sister is a dentist in Atlanta, and one day I got a call from her regarding purchasing a dental office. She described the office as abandoned, with no patients, located in an office complex with several other dentists. But it was an older building that would require a significant investment to bring it up to acceptable standards. I said, "Well, why would you want it?"

Her answer was that the owner was willing to do owner financing and wasn't asking a lot for it. That sent up red flags for me, so I told her to ask herself this series of questions. I share them with you so that you can use them anytime you're considering purchasing a practice:

1. "Is this an A, B+, B-, or C location? If it does not fit the model, why do I want it?"
2. "If money was no object, would I still want it?"
3. "Is a low price affecting my judgment?" Don't get lulled into someone else's disaster just because it's cheap. It's always easy to get into a trap, but can be hell extracting yourself.
4. "Does it fit my ideal office prototype?" You should have one. If not, you're working without a plan.
5. "Can this location produce the cash flow I need?"
6. "Have I done a viability and feasibility study on this practice?"
7. "Did I consult with an experienced financial advisor about this opportunity?"

There are a lot of other questions that you should ask before you commit to a location, but make sure you at least answer these seven before you proceed. Stay focused on your mental model as if it were a franchise and already had a pre-planned look, location, and style to adhere to. Any deviations from your model beyond a B+ should be disqualifying.

Remember, a building is an *asset* only so long as you have patients to turn that space—and the overhead that comes with it—into cash flow. If you can generate a constant flow of patients, it's really hard to go broke in dentistry, even if you're not very good at business. But the minute you stop having those patients, that building becomes a *liability*.

DO

- **Pick a location that meets patient needs.**
- **Choose a highly visible spot.**
- **Work with a real estate lawyer before you sign a lease.**
- **Pay attention to signage, colors, etc.**

How to Choose a Location

When you're trying to choose a location, whether it's for your first independent office or for expansion, always keep this in mind:

The building isn't for you. It's for other people.

The money is for you, but the building is for your patients, and the staff and associates you'll need to hire. It needs to work for them. Here's what I mean:

- **Patients**—Your building needs to be convenient and comfortable for whomever you're targeting. It should be easy to access, whether they are arriving by car, public transit, bike, or on foot. It should be easy to park. It should be easy for patients to get into the building and find your office. People should feel like their cars or bikes will be safe in your parking lot.

- **Associates**—Hiring associates will be a challenge if you're located in an area that's difficult to access or so costly to live in that you shrink your talent pool. Keep the availability of other dentists in mind when you locate.

» **Staff**—The same is true for assistants, clerical staff, bookkeeping staff, etc. Is your building in a spot that makes commuting easy or a nightmare? Is there parking available for employees? The minimum wage just increased and unemployment is at an all-time low. You're going to have to be ready to compete on salaries. You'll need to think of these things.

Plan on taking some time to find a building, whether it's your first or tenth. You'll probably need to look at about 100 to get 10 that you consider serious candidates. Out of those ten, you'll find three that will probably work for you. I used the motto "out of sight, out of mind," and I think it works with everything. If your building is out of sight, no one sees it, but if you have a location that, as soon as you mention it, someone says, "I know exactly where that is," you're golden. You'll also spend less on marketing.

That's especially important in a city like Los Angeles, which has hundreds of these two-level malls on street corners. Half of them have a dental office with a neon sign that just says "Dentist." If you're one of those guys, and you're on the second floor of the back of one of those shopping centers, no one will know you exist. You've got no street visibility.

I've seen new dentists who will settle for those locations because they're cheap. People tell them, "You'll run negative for the first three years, and then you'll start turning a profit." But I didn't want to wait three years for profitability. By the time I opened my doors, I wanted to have the full day booked. I wanted to start turning over patients and making money. So I grabbed a good location right on Hollywood Boulevard—a corner property—put a lot of money out for marketing, and was busy with kids from day one.

Zoning and Other Non-Glamorous Stuff

Before you choose a building, you'll have to consider all kinds of factors about the property itself, starting with zoning. Is the building in an area that's zoned for dental offices? You probably know that in different states and municipalities, the zoning laws are different, but generally, medical and dental facilities are zoned into certain parts of the city. That's why you'll see medical and dental practices, chiropractors, optometrists, pharmacies, diagnostic labs, and hospitals all clustered together a lot of the time.

There are typically three types of zoning districts: residential (R), commercial (C), and manufacturing (M). Then you have density designations. It's all designed to control what can be built where. Before you make a move, go to the zoning office in the city or cities where your buildings are located and find out if they're zoned for medical and dental use. If they're not, forget about them.

Other factors to look at:

» Overall condition
» Square footage
» Power availability
» Traffic patterns
» Parking
» Crime
» Adjacent buildings available for expansion
» Compliance with the Americans with Disabilities Act

Set your radar to look for candidate buildings all the time—when you're out for a run or bike ride, when you're out on the town—or have someone knowledgeable looking for buildings for you. There are real estate agents/brokers who specialize in dental offices, at least in California. Another great resource is www.city-data.com. It's excellent for demographic information.

Over time, you'll develop a sixth sense for properties that fit the bill. If you want to grow, you have to be aggressive and move fast, because the DSOs and big national and multi-national corporations are looking at the same locations, and they already have teams in place to grab them. That's how some of them open four or five locations a month.

I'd suggest finding a real estate broker who knows dental properties—multiple brokers, even—and who could be constantly on the lookout for ideal properties. Give them clear parameters—a certain type of location, a certain size, whatever—and turn them loose. They can bring you buildings around the clock for you to consider. Just make sure everyone's clear on how the broker is getting paid. (Hint: It should be by the lessor when the deal closes, not out of your pocket.)

There are five other major factors to consider when you're looking at a location, especially if it's your first one: *competition*, *patient pool*, *lease*, *build-out*, and *targeting*. I'll hit them one at a time.

Competition

Finding a location for your practice starts with driving around an area that you think you'd like to work in and looking for buildings. Once you find a few candidates, there are a lot of things to think about. One of them is surveying the potential competition.

When you have a location in mind, start looking around for marketing by other dentists. Are you seeing bus bench ads, billboards, signage, direct mailers, or newspaper inserts for other dentists who are targeting the same niche you're targeting? If there are several established dentists in the area, in your niche, and who've been there for a long time, you have two choices:

1. Yield the field and go somewhere else.
2. Change your niche.

Trust me, it's not worth the time or money to try and take market share away from a dentist who is already loved and trusted by the community and "owns" his or her niche. That's like sledding uphill. Now, if a market is overloaded with general dentists, there might be an opportunity to position yourself as a cosmetic dentist, an orthodontist, someone who specializes in seniors, or whatever else makes sense. Look around. What unmet needs do you see? Which population isn't being served?

Keep in mind that if there are very few dentists in an area, there might be a good reason. Maybe it's an ethnic enclave whose members don't trust dentists, or a rural area where homes are remote or few people have dental insurance. There might be ways to leverage conditions like those and profit by serving an underserved population, but you might have to get creative—for instance, using "virtual dental" to reach out to remote areas. A hygienist could go out and take X-rays, do prophys and fluoride treatment, and then send the images to a participating dentist who can do a live diagnosis using the Internet. Be bold and leverage the technology available.

Patient Pool

Can you pull enough patients from the area you're considering to make a profit? And while we're on the subject, can you hire enough associates from nearby areas? I learned about both when I was doing build-outs on three locations up in central California. I went on the Denti-Cal website, which gives you demographic and population information for any area in California, and pulled up Tulare County, a mostly rural area in the state's central valley. And I had to consider hard if I could pull enough people from the surrounding areas with multiple locations, or if I would just be diluting my patient pool.

If I put one location in that area, could I do satellite offices or operate mobile units to serve more patients? How many people could I draw from the surrounding counties, which were very rural? I also had to consider if I would be able to hire associates for those offices, because associates from cities like Bakersfield or Fresno might not be willing to relocate or make the drive, and dentists from cities like L.A. were a lost cause. But I opened an office in Fresno that took off like a rocket. The pent-up demand for a pediatric dentist that would treat Medicaid patients was enormous. It made the other challenges more palatable.

It can be difficult to find dentists who are willing to give up comfort in exchange for wealth. Most would prefer a job down the street from where they live and want to work 9–4, Monday–Thursday, with all weekends off. This is especially true of the dentist whose spouse is also a professional. If you can help them see the big picture—higher pay, support in starting their own offices, etc.—it's easier to recruit them to places that may be less convenient but offer them a chance to make a lot of money.

When you're opening your first office, plan on allocating part of your marketing budget for marketing to dentists, especially if you're in an area that's not popular. You don't have a reputation yet, so you may have to give away some margin to get them—in the form of a sweeter compensation package. Look for people who understand what it means to be an entrepreneur: ambitious people looking for opportunities.

Your Lease

You've chosen a location, have a patient pool nearby that fits your niche, and you've confirmed that the building is zoned for dental. Great. Now you need to lease the building for terms that won't crush you.

My first bit of advice is simple: Know what you can afford each month for a lease to maintain your margins, and rule out any properties higher than that. The second one is simple, too: Work with a real estate attorney and broker to negotiate your lease. Don't do it yourself. You need someone knowledgeable to look over this lease and poke holes in everything. After all, most leases are written by the owners of the property, and once you sign it, you're locked in. In Los Angeles, real estate attorneys cost about $375–$575 an hour, and it's money well spent.

Almost every lease that I've had is a *triple net* lease. In a triple net, you're paying all of the expenses: taxes, common-area maintenance costs, and insurance for the owner. Add a build-out and things start to get very expensive, so you want to have a long lease for cost control while you're growing your business and making money.

You'll probably want to sign a ten-year minimum lease, with two five-year renewable periods. It's also vital to negotiate on price, because your lease will probably have a three percent annual increase built in. Also, make sure you have a clause that says at the end of your first ten years, you can renegotiate terms.

Here's a good reason to hire a smart real estate lawyer and pay the $5,000. Early in my career, I was trying out different lawyers, most of whom didn't specialize in real estate, and I was foolish enough to negotiate a lease by myself. Well, I got into a bad lease that I wanted to get out of. But I had signed the contract and the owner had me. When the lease expired, he told me I could either buy the building—and he gave me his price, which was probably two or three times what it was worth—or he would double my lease. I was forced to move. That's a mistake I never made again, but it was an expensive lesson. Learn from my experience: When in doubt, hire the lawyer.

TALK TO THE EXPERT 

Since 2008, as a dental-specific real estate broker for Gold Leaf Group Healthcare Real Estate, I have assisted doctors in opening over 110 dental practices. My biggest pet peeve is when I am referred to as a "space finder." In this day and age, with technology making commercial real estate listings so accessible, your real estate broker should be more than just a space finder. After all, anyone can jump on LoopNet to search for listings or drive down the street jotting down phone numbers from real estate signs. Your broker should be intimately knowledgeable about dental real estate, a powerful resource to guide you through the process of securing your space. He should be able to vet properties before taking you out to see them, eliminating those properties with parking issues, exclusivity clauses preventing you from opening your office, price restrictions, and a litany of other factors that can limit the feasibility of a location. Prime locations suitable for your practice will be hard to come by, and while the dollars and cents of a transaction are important, "tripping over dollars to pick up pennies" can cost you a great location.

Your broker should set appropriate expectations and help develop the right negotiation strategy for each property. Understanding how landlords think and negotiate will be crucial in securing a lease that will protect you throughout the start-up process and during your tenancy. In addition, a well-negotiated lease will also include the necessary provisions for a smooth and successful transition when you eventually sell your practice. While many landlords will provide rental abatement for the construction of your office, this will rarely be enough time for the process of planning, permitting, and building your dental office. The pre-planning and planning processes should commence well before your lease is signed, so that when you do sign a lease, you can be sure to be open for business prior to the expiration of your rental abatement period.

An experienced, dental-specific broker understands this, and will be an effective project manager, helping you and your team of contractors, designers, attorneys, and lenders efficiently prepare for a successful and seamless office opening. Your broker will be your project manager, helping you and your team of contractors, designers, attorneys, and lenders efficiently prepare for a successful and seamless office opening. In short, don't go shopping for an office location without an experienced dental-specific real estate broker on your team. You can learn more about the process of identifying and securing great dental spaces by going to www.dentalspacesearch.com.

—RJ Przebinda, Co-founder and Principal, Gold Leaf Group, Pasadena, California[18]

Build-Out

You've signed the lease and now you're ready to go. Next, you'll need to turn this blank building into a dental office. Understand going in that build-out will probably cost you from $100 to $200 per square foot (not including equipment costs), depending on the location and the type of work that needs to be done to bring the building up to code and get it patient-ready.

For the build-out, work with dental design companies who specialize in build-outs for dental offices. They're easy to find online and they know exactly what a dentist needs, which you can't say about a general contractor that doesn't work with dentists.

As you get into the design and building phase, know what you need to appeal to your niche. I was marketing to families, so, as I said, I wanted

18 Email interview, November 18, 2018.

to appeal to kids and parents alike. I wanted bright colors so that everyone knew I was a pediatric practice. I had to have parking. I had to have something that was easy to access with a stroller, and a door that a mother carrying a baby could open easily. I wanted the exterior well-lit so that patients would feel safe coming into the parking lot on dark winter evenings.

If I hadn't been targeting kids and families, my build-out might have been very different. Design your building and your space for your niche. If you're selling $2,000 crowns, you can be on the twenty-eighth floor in a building with a marble foyer in Beverly Hills. If you're targeting seniors, you might want more handicapped parking spaces, halls wide enough for walkers, and brighter lights, so that weaker eyes can read paperwork or magazines. Your job is to create the "three C's": *convenience*, *comfort*, and *confidence*. Your space should make it easy for the patient to end up in your chair, make her feel comfortable at every step, and give her confidence that you're a top-flight professional operation.

Targeting

Targeting happens when your build-out is mostly done. It's the stage when you're adding the small touches to the space, inside and out, that will appeal to your unique audience. You can target people with your signage, your interior design, your plant choices, your amenities, your patient perks—all kinds of things.

For example, part of the Kids Dental Kare targeting was our rocking-horse logo, which was visible on every building. Now, faced with that logo or a vanilla sign that says "Dentist," which would you choose? If you're doing a lot of business with Millennials or professionals, and you have fast Wi-Fi and charging ports for people's smartphones, they'll love you.

The other big thing to me that every dental office should be is *clean.*

You're asking people to come to a place that should be sterile and disease-free, so every square inch of the property should make that impression. When I was building my business, I studied the McDonald's model, and I learned that Ray Kroc was a fanatic about cleanliness. I became the same way. If I pulled my car into the parking lot and saw some paper in the parking lot, I picked it up. This was my business and I would do what I needed to, even the small things.

Once, some guy was throwing up in front of the door of one of my offices, and nobody was cleaning it up. I grabbed a bucket and cleaned it up, and I taught my people a lesson in the process: *If the boss has to do this, you'd better get off your butt.* When someone walks into your office, you want them to be impressed, confident, and comfortable.

KEEP IN MIND

- **Learn from dentists who are already successful.**
- **Copy the national brands.**
- **Walk away from what's not working.**

Don't Start from Scratch

Putting the time and money into getting the right location will help you grow a lot faster. You won't spend as much time or money telling people how to find you, you'll get more walk-in traffic, and you'll benefit from the good impression that a nice location and a nice building make because patients will refer their friends and family.

That said, don't go it alone. There are many successful dentists, and as long as you're not a competitor, they'll usually share what they know with you. Most people like to be asked to offer advice, and I think you'll be surprised how readily many dentists will help an up-and-comer. You should also read dental blogs like *Academy of General Dentistry*, *DentalBuzz*, *New Dentist Now*, and *Dental Geek*. The Internet is packed with blogs, forums, and useful articles where you can find lots of information.

Also, emulate the big national brand DSOs like Allied Dental, Heartland Dental, or Pacific Dental Services. They choose the same ideal corner locations in middle- and low-income communities that I've recommended, and for good reason: Those locations are profitable. Copy what the national brands do with build-out, signage, online presence, marketing, and so on, and you can create a brand that looks like a million bucks.

Finally, not all locations will work out. Even if you really want a space, don't let your ego prevent you from walking away from something that's not working. I speak from experience.

I met a dentist who had a location that he was getting frustrated with, and he wanted to work for me. Since his name was on the lease, I said, "Doc, let's do an option. I'll do a lease with you and I'll take over the office for a year, and if it's going well, I have the option to buy everything from you. If not, you can take it back." So we did that deal.

At the end of the year, not only did he want the office back, I wanted to give it back. I had nine or ten offices at that time and a successful system, but that location just didn't take off. It was barely breaking even. I cut bait and moved on.

I didn't do that with what turned out to be the worst location I ever had. It was on a frontage road, and you couldn't even see it from the freeway. But I was determined to make it work, and my ego got in the way. Big mistake. I managed to sell it cheap to a first-time doctor who wanted a location and was thrilled that it was already a dental office. So I was lucky.

Don't rely on luck. Your own ego will trick you. Bury it. You can talk yourself into something because you want it to be right, but that's a bad idea. Have your plan and trust your plan. If something looks good but it deviates from your plan, walk away.

Also, don't get cheap when it comes to getting the right location and spending the money to be competitive. While you're doing things on the cheap, people will walk past you to get to the good-looking new office down the street that meets their expectations. One of my dental school professors used to say, "You can't save your way to being rich: You have to earn it."

Dentistry, like anything, has its successes and failures. But building a business is a long game, so remember, when things are going well, don't get too excited, and when they're not, don't get too low.

As you can see, I've had my share of failures, but I kind of baked that into the cake. Not that I'm expecting an office to fail, but I knew that not everything would go as planned, so I was prepared to hit and get over obstacles. You don't have to win every battle to win the war, but you definitely want to go in intending to win. During the Gulf War, General Norman Schwarzkopf made a statement about preparation that stuck with me: "We want to go in with an overwhelming preponderance of power." Damn, I love that statement. Put together your power team.

EYEING THE EXIT

Your physical locations and the assets tied up in them will be a large part of what an investor buys when you sell your practice. That's why, at some point, it makes sense for you to own the building your office is housed in.

continued

Obviously, that won't always be possible if an office is in a mall or a high-rise. But for offices located in stand-alone buildings, converted residential properties, and the like, buying can be a very smart idea.

You could also build your own office from the ground up, but you should only do that with the assistance of an experienced real estate broker, a commercial developer, and a banker. Your real estate broker will help you locate and value the right property. A developer will tell you how buildable the land is and let you know about possible future development nearby, such as homes (good) or storage units (bad). A banker will let you know what kind of funds you can access for the project.

Bottom line, owning your own buildings is a great idea—sometimes. As with all things, it depends. Consult professionals and remember that your business has many other assets that make it valuable, such as your equipment, your brand, your patient base, and your database.

CHAPTER 4

Market Like Your Life Depends on It . . . Because It Does

CHECK YOUR GPS

If you've chosen your niche, you're one step closer to your million-dollar business. Let's review how far you've come.

- **Deliberately define your destination**: What's your plan for choosing a location or locations? Do you know your criteria and how you'll use locations to target your ideal patients? If you've already chosen a building, do you know how it's zoned?
- **Lock it into your internal GPS**: Line up the experts you'll want on your team in order to make the right choices: a real estate broker, a real estate lawyer, and perhaps a builder or contractor.
- **Choose an ETA**: What's your timeline for build-out and move-in? Keep in mind that from the time you sign a lease, you'll need at least six months for the typical building to be ready, unless it's already a dental office.
- **Devise your plan**: How will you customize your location to appeal to your target patients?

continued

- » **Get started now**: Make your wish list, get demographic and population data, and get online to start scouting neighborhoods and commercial centers. Try LoopNet.com for scouting commercial properties.
- » **Trust the plan and keep moving.**

I'm a marketer and salesman from my college days. I waited tables, sold suits, and sold books door-to-door, and I loved every minute of it. When I got accepted to dental school, I already had the goal of becoming an Entrepreneur Dentist. But since I went to school on scholarship, I had that four-year work obligation—so I used it to my advantage. Those four years gave me time to not only hone my skills as a dentist, but to also study business at the same time.

However, there weren't a lot of courses back in the 1980s designed for dentistry. So I studied other business successes. What I learned changed everything for me, and this was the most important thing I learned:

Marketing is the lifeblood of the dental business.

Marketing brings in patients, and if you have a constant flow of new patients, they will generate revenues for you, provided you can deliver the services you are promoting. The only thing you have to do is follow through with good service, which will lead to referrals, and the cycle continues. However, in dentistry, I found myself spending a lot of time training people in marketing: They would assume that because I had a marketing department, they didn't need to worry about marketing.

That's wrong. Marketing is *everything* you do. How you pick your location. How you address your niche. But it is very difficult to convince dentists, assistants, receptionists, and management that everyone belongs to the marketing department in some way. Start early. Bake that idea into your culture. *Everything is marketing.* Your written messaging. Your visual brand and logo. Everything you do makes an impression, and that's marketing.

In dentistry, marketing has four purposes:

1. Let people know your practice exists and get them to initiate contact.
2. Communicate the special value you offer to your niche.
3. Make people feel comfortable and confident about you.
4. Get patients to refer you to friends and family.

Mailers, billboards, Facebook ads, and all the rest can accomplish the first one, but the look, feel, voice, and service that people experience when they come into contact with your dental business—even when they drive by your building—will do the rest. You've got to pay attention to everything, because you never know what can cost you a patient if you become complacent.

Let me illustrate what I mean. Growing up in the South, I've eaten soul food since day one. But I'm disappointed that, oftentimes, the people who run some soul food joints don't put money back into the business. They seem to take the black community's business for granted. I was in Dallas for the NDA convention, and some guys I was with invited me to go to this soul food place for lunch; when we arrived, there was a long line of people out the door. But there were flies on the windowsill, the tables were sticky, and the bathroom was disgusting. It said to me, "We don't care about our customers because we know they'll come back." I left. Soul food I can find, and I'm not going to give my business to a place that's so clueless.

In marketing, you can't rest. If that seems overwhelming, it doesn't have to be. Let's look at how to manage your marketing, so that you can build something big.

Trying Everything

When I started Kids Dental Kare, my marketing consisted of, well, everything. You don't always know what's going to work at first, so you try it all. In general, for dentistry, I divide marketing into three rough categories:

» **Category One**—Visibility marketing, including outdoor ads, bus bench ads, newspaper ads, and direct mailers, lets the people in your niche know you're out there.

» **Category Two**—Relationship marketing is about getting people to know, like, and trust you, which mostly means going into the community, talking to and educating people, and reaching out to other dentists and physicians in the area to build trust and get referrals.

» **Category Three**—Maintenance marketing mostly consists of creating email offer campaigns aimed at current patients (to get more referrals), sending out Christmas cards, etc. You're letting them know they're appreciated so that they keep coming back.

Early on, I had nineteen or twenty marketing activities going simultaneously, including advertising, presentations at elementary schools, speaking at community centers and leaving collateral, hiring outside reps to talk to other dentists to build my professional referral base, and so on. If the Internet had been a thing, I would've been working that, too.

In the beginning, you try everything because marketing is the rocket fuel for your business, and you're building from scratch. Over time, by tracking where your patients come from, you'll see what gives you the best ROI and you can drop some of your less productive marketing channels.

One thing I found was that, because my niche was pediatrics, the more personal my marketing was, the better my results. After I ran my Armenian ads in Russian on local television, the local station aimed at the Armenian community asked me if I wanted to do a commercial for them in Russian.

So I did. Then I was invited to the Armenian dental society meeting, and everyone knew me because I had been marketing and advertising to the community. Two guys came over to me during that event and they wanted to know my secret. How did I break into the Armenian community and get so many of them as patients? I said, "Well, they like me and trust me with their kids." It was that simple. I'd talked to them, respected their language, and connected with them.

I also sent out a simple, but very, very effective, letter to all the doctors in the area that said something like this: "Hi, I'm Dr. Jerry Lanier, a general dentist that has a practice limited to kids. If you have any kids with behavior management problems that you prefer not to treat, I would like to be a resource for you." It generated a lot of referrals.

- **Your marketing needs to make a consistent impression.**
- **Marketing is an investment in your business and future.**
- **It's always a good idea to hire an outside marketing firm.**

What Your Marketing Should Say

The tactics you use in your marketing will depend on the niche you're targeting, your budget, and your personal preferences, but the basics of any dental office's messaging will be roughly the same. There are two levels of messaging: *literal* and *implicit*. Literal messaging is communicated through copy and tells prospective patients the basics: who you are, where you are, what services you offer, your hours, discounts for first-time patients, and so on.

Implicit messaging is communicated more through design, photos, and even the quality of paper you use in your brochures or direct mailers. It should communicate that your practice is a professional operation, that you're experts in your areas of specialization, that you respect the patient and appreciate their business, and that they can refer friends and family and know they'll be taken care of.

As far as what kind of messaging and graphics your niche will respond to, that's where research comes in. There are a lot of companies that will sell you expensive market research reports on all sorts of demographic groups, but those are a waste of your money. The best market research is getting to know the group you're trying to reach and finding out what they care about.

If you're leasing an expensive suite in a high-rise in a wealthy area, it's a safe bet that your marketing will need to look and feel first-class, like a brochure you might pick up in a BMW dealership. The messaging will be about concierge-level service and convenience, and the photography might evoke the feeling of being at a spa. You won't breathe a word about discounts or specials, because your audience equates value with price.

On the other hand, let's say you're targeting a particular part of your city. You're going to want to learn as much as you can about the people who live there—and I don't just mean their ethnicity, income, and other basics like that, though those are important. You'll want to attend community events and talk to people about what's happening in the area. You'll want to look at other dental practices in the neighborhood, find out why the successful ones have succeeded, and figure out what killed the ones that closed. Is there a high school football team everyone's crazy about? Is there a respected local business owner or city councilperson whose brain you can pick?

Sometimes this isn't that labor intensive, especially if you pick the right niche. Because I was focused on kids, I could assume a few things. Parents wanted my office to be convenient, they wanted me to take their insurance, and they wanted to know that I would take great care of their little angels. As long as I reinforced that message with their in-office experience, I usually got and kept their business.

You can safely assume any audience will want messaging that suggests convenience, friendly service, cleanliness, and professionalism. However, it's dangerous to assume too much beyond that. If you do, you're making bets that you might lose. That's why I recommend balancing more traditional marketing methods, such as advertising, with personal outreach visits to senior living homes, schools, or community centers. It's more time consuming, but you'll connect with people personally and learn a lot.

"Nobody cares how much you know 'til they know how much you care."

—ZIG ZIGLAR

Create a Patient Experience

My marketing journey started while I was in college working many service jobs: waiting tables, delivering room service, and selling men's clothing. When you're used to working for tips, you understand the importance of getting into character and training on scripts. It's rewarding to work for tips or commissions because you know that you have to influence people's decision-making—and do it with such flair and subtlety that they believe you deserve a tip. I always got a rush out of closing a sale or convincing someone to say yes to what I was offering.

The same was true with my patients. I'd don my dentist persona, Dr. Friendly, and go to work "earning my tips." I had rehearsed my lines and my whole demeanor: body language, hand gestures, you name it. Everything was designed to deliver the best effect, and to get a positive response from the patient. Done right, by a well-rehearsed team—from the front-desk staff to dental assistants and X-ray techs, all using a coordinated script—it made the overall experience pleasant and unique and far exceeded patients' expectations.

The patient experience you plan and execute is the key to your marketing. It involves every part of what your customer will encounter, from the name of your practice and the appearance of your logo to photos of your office and your page ranking on Google. And these are only what they see of you online, before they even hear your telephone reception and enjoy your in-office atmosphere. Don't take for granted any aspect of what a patient experiences at any point of contact with your business, no matter how small.

The second key here is to train all your people and have them on a script. Never assume that anyone will intuitively know how to conduct themselves according to your vision or relate to patients in the way you want them to. You have to tell them your vision. Make it available for everyone to read or watch on video. Have your people go through training, quiz them on the customer experience, and help them role-play it until they own it.

As you grow, this will become more and more difficult, because the message will get diluted as it passes down from you through more and more hands. That's why it's vitally important to create an online portal that holds all of your training materials, videos, and applications. You will not have time to personally train each new hire. If you're going to offer a consistent experience, you must have a system for training, testing, retraining, and retesting everyone on all of your standard operating procedures.

That includes your associate dentists, who are usually the hardest ones to convince. In fact, unless the talent pool in your area is very shallow, I suggest that you be up-front with potential associates about their need to embrace your marketing mindset, and that if they won't get on board, you won't hire them.

Invest in Your Marketing

One thing you cannot do is think of marketing as an optional activity. It is *essential.* I have seen well-located dental practices run by talented, personable dentists flop miserably because the dentist in charge didn't think marketing was a necessary expense. Usually, they had clung to the belief that because they were so proud of their practice and thought it was the greatest thing since the iPhone, everyone else would feel the same way. But that's self-delusion.

Look at it this way. Ever heard of Nike? McDonald's? Budweiser? They're huge global brands that everyone knows, but they still run commercials and do all kinds of other marketing. Why? Because they have competitors, and because people face a lot of distractions. If those giant brands still have to market, so do you. Think of patient awareness and loyalty as something heavy, like a barbell that you have to keep lifting all the time. That's what your marketing does.

How much should you plan on spending on your marketing? A good rule of thumb for a dental business is fifteen percent of your gross annual revenues. So if you have one office and it brought in $600,000 in revenue last year, you should plan on spending $90,000 on marketing-related activities next year. Here are some of the things you might use that money for:

- Graphic design
- Logo design
- Copywriting

- Photography
- Printing
- Postage
- Ad space
- Video production costs
- Premiums and giveaways
- Website design
- Signage
- Email services
- Google AdWords
- Special events
- Commissions to sales reps

If you're launching a brand-new dental business or moving to a market where you're unknown, bump that number up to twenty to twenty-five percent. You'll need to spend extra to let people know you've arrived and to show them where to find you—and, of course, to overtake entrenched competitors. My advice is to build that percentage into your monthly budget and forget about it. It's a permanent cost of doing business until the day you sell your company and walk away. Treat it as essential, because it is.

DO

- **Choose a wide selection of marketing tactics.**
- **Track results to assess a tactic's ROI.**
- **Pay attention to online reviews and Google searches.**
- **Make sure your patient experience is unmatched, every time.**

Your Most Important Marketing Tactics

Of course, you can't do everything. So it's important to know which marketing tactics are most important for dentists and which are either outdated or ineffective. This is what worked for me over the years:

» **Online reviews**—Internet marketing almost pulled the rug out from under me when it came along in earnest. I wasn't prepared for it, and there were young dentists who'd grown up with it who were eating my lunch. Don't let that happen. You need to pay attention to reviews in three online locations: Yelp, Google, and Facebook. Yelp reviews can be tainted, so you have to watch out for that, but you still need to solicit positive reviews from as many patients as you can.

My wife finally got me to pay more attention to reviews because she's a review reader. I said to her, "Brenda, some people just post because they don't like somebody." But she understood what was really going on and she said, "If this is all I have to go off of, I'm going by the reviews." She was right. Fair or not, I couldn't ignore reality. According to marketing data firm BrightLocal, forty-nine percent of customers need a four-star rating before they will choose a local business.[19]

I finally hired someone full-time to work just on online marketing, and he spent half of his time asking for reviews and chasing down unfair ones. But you have to take control of the narrative about your business, because if you don't, someone else will. Have a process: Provide stellar service; ask the patient for a review in the office; then send them an email or text the next day asking for the review.

---

19 BrightLocal, "2018 Local Consumer Review Survey," www.brightlocal.com/learn/local-consumer-review-survey/#local-business-review-habits, accessed September 28, 2018.

» **Google and SEO**—Today, when someone searches for a dentist, odds are they're doing it on Google. So you need your practice to appear in the first page of search results, because nobody goes to the second page. That requires *search engine optimization*, or SEO. SEO means having someone seed the text on your website, and the underlying "tags," with words that people are likely to use in their Google searches. So, if you're a pediatric dentist serving, say, Bainbridge Island, Washington, you would want to have phrases like "Bainbridge Island children's dentist" and "Bainbridge dentist for kids" scattered throughout your website.

The other part of Google you should be on top of is Google AdWords. You know those paid results at the top of most Google search results pages? Businesses buy them by buying AdWords using an auction system. The more your link gets clicked on, the more you pay, but that's okay because you're getting real leads on new patients. Go to ads.google.com for all the information you need about leveraging AdWords.

» **Your website**—Logically, the next thing you should be thinking about in this age of online marketing is your dental website. Today, websites are much more than simple online brochures: They're the centerpieces of your brand. So, they have to make a great impression, with beautiful photography and graphic design that captures the personality of your practice. But they should also be useful, allowing visitors to learn about your dentists, read about the services you offer, pre-register for appointments, enter their dental history, book appointments online, sign up for your e-newsletter, read articles (about everything from preparing for anesthesia before oral surgery to caring for braces and retainers), and even look for jobs.

Today, your website is your storefront. It's the first place people will look for information about your dental office, and they will judge you based on the site's look, feel, utility, and functionality. There are plenty of web development shops that specialize in websites for dentists, so finding a vendor shouldn't be an obstacle. Also, because so many people access the web on their mobile devices, make sure your website is optimized for both tablets and smartphones.

» **Social media**—I was way behind the curve on social media, which wasn't as big a deal for my business back in the early days because I was appealing to parents, who weren't as dependent on social media then. But today, parents and young people alike are using social media to find businesses, read reviews, and get information about dentists and dentistry, so you have to be on the various services.

My suggestion is that you outsource your social media to an individual or small agency, because social media is most effective when you post every day. You should be on the "Big Three": Facebook, which is best for reaching parents and people over forty with articles and information; Twitter, best for posting things like daily dental tips, as well as links to dental articles; and Instagram, perfect for reaching young people with photos of patients at your offices, special events, etc.

Social media is not a sales medium. Instead, make your posts useful: coupons, links to oral health information, community news, or funny videos related to teeth—things like that. Use social media to engage and build relationships.

» **Email**—Use every opportunity you can to build your email list. Ask people to give you their email address when they come to your website, book an appointment, subscribe to your blog (if you have one), sign in at your office, and finish up their appointment. Give them the incentive of getting an e-newsletter full of information, news, and *special offers*.

Use an service like MailChimp or Constant Contact to create and distribute a regular e-newsletter to your patients. Sending it monthly is fine, though if you can manage to do it weekly, that would be better. Make the content personable and informational, like you're talking to an old friend who you want to keep informed.

» **Publishing articles**—It took me a while, but I started writing articles about all sorts of things parents needed to know related to pediatric dentistry; I published them on my WordPress site and on LinkedIn. After a while, if someone searched for a children's dentist, my articles would pop up. It's better (and a *lot* cheaper) than advertising, because it's unpaid and more credible. If you're only running one office and have some writing chops, you could write such things yourself, but I'd recommend farming that work out to a freelancer. Find a professional writer you can talk to regularly about article ideas (or someone you can just post notes for on a platform like Google Docs). Put out a couple of good articles a month, on topics relevant to your niche, and you'll get results.

» **Community presence**—Get into the community in any way you can and let people get to know you. Like I said before, I would go into schools and do presentations. I hired a rep to go to community groups and give out information. I did live remotes with local radio stations. I'd pay a sponsorship fee, and the radio station would advertise where we would be. We'd put up tents and fly balloons; there would be face painting and clowns—the whole scene.

Once, we were over in east L.A., in a neighborhood called Boyle

Heights. This radio station had a big toy giveaway every Christmas, and families would line up a day before and stay there all night waiting on these toys. I got to be a part of that, which is a good feeling, because you get a chance to hang out with the people in the community. You spend the night out there with them and you really bond. That type of thing is worth $100,000 in marketing, especially when you're targeting families.

You don't need any special representative or system to do community work, only a nice, professional brochure and maybe a slide show. Just reach out to community centers, senior centers, school districts, local hospitals—whatever suits your target niche.

Referrals

I put referrals last and all by themselves because they are the most important part of any dentist's marketing, and I want you to remember what I've written about them. Referrals are gold, not only because they're free but also because they come with an endorsement: "See my dentist, Dr. So-and-So, he's wonderful." The person receiving the referral is very likely to call for an appointment, and if you take care of them, you might have another referral source, too.

You should also be leveraging relationships with other dentists and health-care providers in the area. Contact them and let them know that you'll happily return the favor if they refer patients who fit your niche.

There are three aspects to a good patient referral program:

1. ***Ask for the referral.*** A man could die of thirst in the middle of a lake if he never asks for water. Some dentists won't ask for the referral, but if you provide great service, and your patients have a consistently good

experience, you're crazy not to ask. If patients are happy, they will refer others to you for as long as you keep them happy. So ask. Ask after the appointment. Ask in your e-newsletter. Ask on your website. Just say, "If you liked your experience and you have family or friends who might be looking for a dentist, would you please refer them?"

2. ***Incentivize and facilitate referrals.*** Sometimes, my patients would brag, "Doctor, I've already referred six friends to you." You're building a referral machine, so you have to reward the people who make it work. If somebody is sending you enough patients, you ought to give them some flowers or something. For some reason, some dentists think it's illegal to reward people for referrals, but that's untrue. You could create a loyalty program where patients earn points for each person they refer, and after earning a certain number of points, they get a discount on their next dental procedure—or even something unrelated, like a gift card for a nice local restaurant. That's perfectly fine, and I recommend it.

   You should also make it as easy as possible for your patients to provide referrals. Give them a stack of brochures, business cards, or special first-time patient coupons, or have a referral website with its own web address, where referred patients can go for a unique experience.

3. ***Have a program to care for referral patients.*** You'll only get a second referral from a patient if you treat the first one like gold. So create a special program to take special care of a referred patient on his or her first visit. You don't have to give them champagne and feed them grapes, but a special "Welcome to our practice" basket wouldn't be a bad idea. Make them feel like kings or queens before, during, and after their initial visit.

Other Marketing You Can Try

Of course, that's far from everything you can try as you figure out what works best for your business. I've tried many strategies over the years, some more effective (and cost-effective) than others.

Television advertising can be effective if you can target it very narrowly, but it's very expensive. You're talking about not only buying the airtime but also paying for production. Radio advertisement isn't bad, but the same principle applies: If you target a specific group, like I did with my Russian TV spots for Armenians, you can get a nice ROI. Otherwise, for radio, it's probably better to do things like live remotes and event sponsorships.

Online video is a wonderful tool. If I had it to do over again, I might produce and release one YouTube video a week about all sorts of topics related to kids dentistry: keeping kids from being afraid; how to brush and floss properly; you name it. Video is effective and it goes viral more easily than anything else. If you like being on camera and have ideas for videos that are clever and informative, try it out. Just make sure your production values are good, particularly the quality of the sound. Bad sound quality makes even the best online videos impossible to watch.

Outdoor advertising on billboards and bus benches is still very common in cities, but it's expensive and I don't know that it gives you a lot of bang for the buck. Plus, signing a contract for an outdoor ad is a huge commitment. Once, I was paying about $30,000 for a series of outdoor ads when some bad advice from an accountant resulted in me getting hit with a huge penalty from the IRS. Suddenly, I couldn't afford those outdoor ads, but I was under contract, and the people who sold me the ads wanted their money. That was rough.

If you're new to an area, outdoor can be useful for getting your name out. But once you're established, you're better off using your funds for referral programs and online advertising.

Finally, you'll need business collateral—brochures and business cards. Make them classy and attractive; hire a professional designer. Don't DIY your collateral, or your business will appear cheap and second-rate. Everything makes an impression, and you want that impression to be a good one because there are a lot of dentists out there.

KEEP IN MIND

- **Everything you do is marketing.**
- **Your in-office experience can make or break you.**
- **You're always building a brand.**

Everything You Do Is Marketing

I've been talking about tools because it's important for you to know about the basics, but that can be misleading. The truth is, everything you do in and around your dental business is marketing, because it will all affect how your patients see you, either positively or negatively.

You've heard of the term *branding*, right? Well, when you execute your marketing strategy for your dental business, you're building a brand. What is a brand? Basically, it's a promise that says "This is what I stand for" and "This is what I will always deliver." Your brand creates expectations for your patients, your associates, your staff, and the community.

Once you establish it, everything you do either supports those expectations or contradicts them. Support them and you'll have happy patients, lots of referrals, and lots of growth. Contradict them and you'll create ill will and probably lose patients.

That's why you have to develop an "I'm always marketing" mindset. The motto "Out of sight, out of mind" works for marketing as well as choosing a location, because if you're out of sight, you're out of your customer's mind and you're out of business. You've got to find a way to tickle someone's brain cells and tell them "I'm here for you." They may not have a need for your services at that moment, but when the need arises, you need to be top of mind. When I was running my business, Kids Dental Kare was visible constantly in the community; I was always on parents' minds when they thought about dentistry.

I marketed so constantly that it got to the point where I was locally famous. Once, a guy walked into my office with his son. I was a general dentist doing pediatrics, but I had hired a guy two years out of USC who was a pediatric specialist. The office was getting very busy; I was giving him some of my patients; we were rocking and rolling . . . and then this family came in and wanted to see me. I was slammed, so I talked to the father and told him I had this young dentist who was really great, and he would work on the man's son. But the father wasn't having it. He said, "But I want *you* to see my child. I saw you on TV. I trust you." That's what media does. For better or worse, when people see you everywhere, they trust you.

But this marketing mindset really pivots on the experience people have when they come into your office and interact with your physical environment, dentists, and staff. You can have a great website, beautiful ads, and a gorgeous building, but if patients feel ignored, disrespected, or treated poorly in any way, you've blown the ballgame in the bottom of the ninth.

Nothing about your office environment should be left to chance or accidental. You and your practice manager (if you have one) should design every activity and interaction to be welcoming, positive, and efficient. Every time a patient speaks with one of your staff, that's a chance to connect with them and build affinity.

Nobody Cares How Much You Know . . .

While the well-known Zig Ziglar quote is deep, it's also true. You really have to show patients that you care, and that's even more important when you're working with kids. Parents have to feel, at every stage of their interaction, that this is a caring group of people they can trust with their baby.

But it doesn't matter if you're working with kids, seniors, or anyone in between. When patients walk in the door, they should hear, "Hi, good morning. How are you today?" The patient should instantly command your receptionist's full attention; he or she shouldn't be typing away or shoving paperwork in the patient's face. But all too often, that's what happens. You have to train on this stuff. When you walk into a Starbucks and the baristas greet you with a genuine-sounding "Hi! Welcome to Starbucks!" that doesn't happen by accident. That's how they're trained. That's a part of the Starbucks brand.

Everything—including the condition of your office, your signage and your building, the efficiency of your intake process, the music you pipe in, how you follow up after procedures, and how your people handle problems and complaints—is all marketing. It should all feel intentional and designed. Train your people to understand that they are part of your marketing efforts—that marketing isn't just something that people in an outside agency do. They are part of the face of your business, and what they do matters.

By the way, the most important person in your business when it comes to your marketing is—you guessed it—*you*. You are the most important ambassador of your brand. Whenever you're dealing with patients or the public, you have to bring your A game. From the time I walked in to see a patient (and his or her parent), I was on stage. I would play to the mom, because the first thing she needed to think was "Wow, this guy's good with kids."

I would do my little song and dance with the child, making him or her feel at ease, asking questions, telling them what we were going to be doing and why, and that there was nothing to fear. Meanwhile, I knew the parent was watching my every move. I was performing for them and selling them, and often, the next thing I knew, they would be hugging me. I had my routine, my patter, and it never varied. It's like when I used to wait tables; when you're back in the kitchen you can play around, but once you push that curtain back, you're on.

Sometimes, to earn a patient's loyalty, all you need to do is learn a few words in their native language or a few cultural subtleties that indicate respect. I don't speak a lot of Spanish, but I learned enough to tell parents what I was going to do, and they *loved* that I cared enough to speak to them in their native tongue.

The doctors you hire are a close second in importance. They need to be more than technicians because dentistry is personal. They need to be able to at least do the song and dance, but it's better if they're skilled and also personable. I had a doctor work for me for a little while, and he was really good. But he was an older white guy and he did not care for Latinos. One day, a Hispanic mom was in the treatment room with her son, and he just walked in, didn't say anything to the mom or child, and just did the exam. When he was done, he got up, dropped everything, and walked out, leaving the assistant to explain to Mom what was going on with her son's teeth. It was awful.

After the appointment, the mom took me aside and said, "I like your office and I love your service and the girls, but this doctor's an asshole. Don't ever let him see my kid again." Message received, loud and clear.

Your associates need to, at the least, be reasonably skilled at relating to patients and putting them at ease. Some patients will get emotional; children get flat-out scared. The dentist is there to help them cross the burning sands. Some docs will insist that chairside manner is "something you have to be born with," but that's nonsense. Anyone can learn the basics of being cordial and welcoming to a patient, even if they have to fake it. If an associate can't at least do the song and dance and make patients feel welcome, respected, and safe, they're going to do more harm to your business than good.

TALK TO THE EXPERT 

It is critical to the success of a dental practice to develop a strategic marketing plan that clearly defines the patient population being targeted. The planning process depends on understanding that population in order to reach the type of new patients that the practice is looking for. This will ensure a solid foundation for the marketing strategy and produce long-term results.

The Kids Dental Kare strategic marketing and branding plan was developed to target populations in communities that had limited access to pediatric dental services. The target audience was mothers with young children who had government-funded dental benefits. Some other tips:

- » Because marketing resources are limited, it is important to select the most cost-effective advertising channels. A marketing director must understand the demographics of the advertising channels in order to obtain the desired results. I have used radio, direct mail, social media, and other channels to market health-care services. It has been my experience that direct-to-consumer is one of the most effective tactics; localized marketing events give health-care providers the opportunity to promote services directly to the consumer.
- » Following the Golden Rule is the best way to get free press coverage. Over the years, I have coordinated, participated

in, and sponsored local charitable events that have benefited thousands of children in California, and that has yielded tens of thousands of dollars' worth of free press coverage.

» The best way to save money on the printing and production of marketing collateral is to have a professional relationship with a quality graphic artist who understands your strategic marketing and branding plan and can design materials that are economical to print.

—BRENT EDWARDS, HEALTHCARE MARKETING SOLUTIONS[20]

Your Marketing System

The best way to exercise some control over this chaotic mix of people, materials, media, strategies, and procedures is to create a marketing system that controls as much of your marketing activity as possible. You're probably starting to get bleary-eyed with all this talk of marketing, so I'll cut right to the chase. Here's what to do:

» **Automation**—Get your marketing as automated as possible, so that email, mailers, and social media posts go out like clockwork. Tools like Hootsuite let you schedule social media content; other automation might just be a matter of keeping writers and other service providers on schedule. Create a master schedule for all your marketing for each quarter, and at the end of the quarter, evaluate what worked and what

20 Email interview, September 24, 2018.

should be changed or discontinued. Use cloud-based scheduling tools like CoSchedule to keep everyone on the same page.

» **Consistency**—Ensure consistency in everything that the public sees. Make sure your logo is the same everywhere. Standardize your staff's phone interactions by training them on a phone script for greetings, appointment reminder calls, follow-up calls, and so on. Use the same tagline everywhere. Make sure your messaging is concise and consistent, covering the same few points about who you serve and the value you create. Make sure everything is consistent from location to location, down to the paint colors and style of waiting-area furniture.

» **Training**—Train your staff on how to interact with patients, talk on the phone, handle problems, and even do specific marketing tasks, such as ordering printing and managing direct mail. Schedule training regularly, even if your people think they know something, because it's human nature to become complacent.

Train your people until following the script becomes like muscle memory, as automatic as sinking a free throw for a basketball player. Train them to smile and say, "good morning" and "thank you" without thinking about it. Also, remind them that they are actors on your stage. When they're at work, they're on. You don't care how they act when they're at home, but when they punch in, they're a representative of your company, and everything they do reflects on you.

» **Repetition**—Marketing takes time to show results. Be persistent. It can take months to start seeing results. Create the system, create the tools, roll them out, and don't worry about results for the first three to six months. Keep yourself in front of your prospective patients as much as you can. The more they see you, the more likely they are to call you.

» **Tracking**—How will you know what's working and what's not unless you track where your patients are coming from? Make it standard procedure to ask patients what brought them into your office. Was it an ad? A mailer? An article on LinkedIn? Did they shake your hand at a community event? Track the *open rate* and *click-through rate* of your email and the number of people who read each online article you publish. What's bringing in the most patients? More important, what's each patient costing you to acquire?

For example, let's say you're paying $10,000 for a billboard and it's bringing in ten new patients a month, based on what the patients say. Not bad. But you're also running ads on Facebook and they're costing you $2,500 a month and bringing in five new patients each month. The billboards are bringing in more business, but your cost of acquisition is $1,000 per patient for outdoor versus $500 for Facebook. Facebook gives you a better ROI.

Become obsessive about tracking and testing everything and comparing costs of acquisition. Keep what's working well and what patients like; shelve the rest. In the end, know what your practice stands for and the values you represent, and stand by them. Your patients will come to you for who you are just as much as what you can do.

EYEING THE EXIT

Document all of your marketing processes. When you come to sell your business, your buyer will want documentation for everything, including—

- » Office procedures
- » Phone and in-person protocols
- » How dentists, hygienists, and staff greet and interact with people
- » Referral programs
- » Direct mail messages
- » E-newsletter procedures
- » Graphic design and other vendors
- » Key contacts at schools, community centers, and radio stations
- » Other dentists you refer or partner with
- » Anything else that relates to your marketing

Documentation will make your business more appealing to a buyer looking for "plug and play" profits.

CHAPTER 5

Build Your Systems

CHECK YOUR GPS

Marketing is the heartbeat of your business. Let's make sure that heart is beating strong.

- **Deliberately define your destination**: What's your projected marketing budget per year, and what kind of year-over-year patient growth do you want that spending to produce?
- **Lock it into your internal GPS**: Choose the array of marketing tactics you'll try in the next year. If you're new to aggressive marketing, try a little of everything so you can see what works: print, online, outdoor, direct mail, email, and community outreach.
- **Choose an ETA**: When will you launch your marketing campaign and how long will you run it before you course-correct?
- **Devise your plan**: What's your overall marketing deployment schedule?
- **Get started now**: Choose vendors for writing, graphic design, web design, logo design, and printing, relying on experts and reviews or referrals whenever possible. Get a production schedule for your marketing tools.
- **Trust the plan and keep moving.**

When I was in high school biology class, I sat near a fellow student whose study habits impressed and intrigued me (and who would go on to complete medical school). People always called Ovida McIntosh a genius, but she'd just smile and reply, "No, I'm not a genius. I study; I have a system!"

One day, Ovida explained her systematic method of learning. She said that she'd always sit in the front of the class and take copious notes. Then, after class, she would go to the library and rewrite all her notes, so she could study them over the next few days. That was how she learned the material so well.

That was a revelation to me. I thought, "I don't have to be a genius to learn this. I just have to follow a system!" So I did. I started doing what Ovida did, action for action, and found that it worked well for me, too. This would be one of my first inklings that *systems* could pave the way to success, and I would apply that lesson years later in building my business.

Systems Make a Practice a Business

Remember this quote: "If you don't have a system, you don't have a business." Who said that? Yours truly. A business operates as a cohesive unit, with everything oriented around a single goal. A practice is just a bunch of dentists, assistants, hygienists, and staff doing their own thing.

Part of your system must include measuring your ROI on everything. If work doesn't contribute to profitability, it's useless. You're not operating a charity. I remember getting into an argument with my marketing guy because he wanted me to pay him for effort, not results. He told me he'd been making calls on doctors, but none of his referrals were showing up. I told him I couldn't pay him based on his effort, because I was hiring him to bring in business. It's like hunting for food. I can tell my family that I tried, but that doesn't fill their bellies.

In the end, if you don't measure it, you can't manage it. I had a big falling out with another marketing manager because he refused to use my management system. I insisted on inputting everything: where patients heard about us, if they had seen ads, if someone had referred them or if they referred someone, and so on. I was spending a lot of time, effort, and money on my marketing, and I needed to know—is it working or not working? He didn't think that was important, and I ended up letting him go because of it.

Systems like ROI reporting are critical to your business because they turn the chaos of operations into actionable data. Systems play three important roles in the development of your dental business:

1. They give you a window into your finances; you can see revenues, expenses, margins, marketing expenditures, marketing ROI, and so on.
2. They automate everything from e-newsletters to patient reminders to billing, so nothing slips through the cracks.
3. They document the critical aspects of your business so that it's relatively turnkey, and therefore desirable, to an investor.

If your goal is to build something that you can sell in the long term, systems are not an option—they're a necessity. No one is going to buy a chaotic dental practice that has no idea what's going in and out each month and can't determine which marketing initiatives are paying off and which aren't. Investors buy profit machines. They care about businesses they can turn into positive cash flow quickly. Systems—automated, trackable, and predictable—are what make your business *saleable* in the long run. They make your business turnkey—so that anyone can invest in it, take over, and start making money right away.

Just as important, systems make you obsolete. If the business is dependent on your hands-on management and your brand to be profitable, no one will buy it—because you don't come with the deal. A saleable franchise is one that can run without the founder. So let's look at the kinds of systems that a dental business needs.

THINK

- **Everything in your office should be part of a process.**
- **You are the CEO; you shouldn't be handling minutiae.**
- **Processes free you to think ahead and think big.**

Don't Improvise—Routinize!

The most important part of any system is creating predictability in the day-to-day operations of your business, especially if you're running a multi-office franchise. There's a reason that going into a Starbucks in Portland, Oregon, or Portland, Maine, is the same experience: The company has left nothing to chance. Everything is standardized. Take your cue from giant brands and do the same thing. Don't improvise. Your business is not the place for creativity.

A set of company-wide procedures is your defense against anyone—dentist, staff member, or assistant—going off the reservation and deciding to do things his or her own way without your knowledge. It's your "This is the way we do things around here" statement. People don't change things on their own at any of your locations; headquarters makes those decisions. If someone wants to try something new, great. They have to run it by you or your practice manager and get it approved, and then they can test it out.

Everything in your offices should be systematic and predictable: how you meet, greet, and dismiss patients; what you say to them; how you sterilize your instruments; when you open a bag—you name it. The focus should be on time, productivity, and balancing service and quality (and the patient's perception of being cared for) with speed and turnover. There should be a procedures manual (it doesn't matter if it's a physical binder or a digital file in the cloud) that dictates the granular steps for dealing with—

» Patients who've been waiting a while;
» Delivery people;
» Complaints;
» Bad reviews;
» People who don't speak English;
» People who have a disability; and
» People who are terrified of the dentist.

If you're building your business the right way, it should be virtually impossible to surprise you or the staff at any of your locations, because you've anticipated almost everything that can happen, designed a procedure to deal with it, tested that procedure, and trained on it exhaustively.

You need this because you can't be in two places at once, much less six or ten. As I wrote earlier, when you get beyond two or maybe three locations, your job changes. You need to be the CEO. Your job is not to run the day-to-day systems. Your job is running the whole business: doing marketing and PR, hiring good people, meeting with lawyers and finance people, and taking care of the big picture.

You're Always the Boss

A system keeps things running your way when you can't have your eyes on every detail. And as you grow, that will be most of the time. You'll be off-site scouting buildings, meeting with bankers, or doing interviews, and you'll need to know that your entire business is on course. You can only allow so much deviation before you're way off track, like targeting a niche that's outside your sweet spot or spending too much on marketing. Any business can drift unless you're constantly checking in, so you put systems in place so you don't *have* to check in as often.

For example, I had a marketing guy who was pretty good when he first came aboard, but I think he just took his job for granted. He drifted. We had scheduled a big public event, and when you do those events, you've got to get there at six in the morning to set up. We had a system and a check sheet, and we thought everything was solid. The day before, someone needed to make sure that we had balloons, accessories, and giveaway items—and that the helium tank was full. My marketing manager and his team were supposed to take care of it, but by the time I got there, it was eight o'clock in the morning and there was nothing on the table. They had forgotten the gift bags. It cost me at least $5,000 to be there, and I gained nothing (on a Saturday) because I didn't have anything to give people.

Part of it was my fault. I got too lax. I got too friendly. I wanted to be pals with everybody, but when you're the boss, you can't get too familiar, or people feel like they can take advantage of you. When you're running a business, you need to be the boss first. You have to give orders, set expectations, and hold people accountable. If you want a friend, get a dog.

But another part of the problem was not having a system that made that kind of mistake nearly impossible to make. If we'd had a setup where there were predetermined jobs, and where more than one person was responsible for ensuring that what needed to go to the remote site got there, that mistake probably wouldn't have happened. Your system is your eyes and ears.

Another important aspect of a good system is that it makes individuals expendable. People can and will quit or flake out, and if you've put a lot of faith and trust in the person who flakes on you, you could be in trouble. I had an IT guy who ran my website, my database, my network—everything. We had some disagreements, but I didn't fire him, because I didn't know what he knew. That made me dependent on him. If I fired him or he got hit by a bus, who would come in to keep things running? I didn't know how the servers worked or how we got Wi-Fi service. I always felt that the reason he wouldn't document his procedures and create a system was due to the job security and leverage it gave him. Luckily, he was a great worker and executed his duties through to the end. But I was scared. If I had it to do over again, I'd make it mandatory that the manual of operations for any department be updated quarterly—especially for IT—because things change quickly, now. Any company of a certain size has to run based on *documented* systems.

Dependence on a human being is unacceptable if you want to build a saleable business. Your business can't be dependent on anyone—*including you*. Everybody should be expendable. Keep in mind that your staff may not be willing to document systems if they don't fully understand how to do it or why it's valuable. Plan on training them on it. And never let on that one of the ideas behind a system is that it makes them expendable. People won't usually commit to something they fear might cost them their jobs.

DO

- **Implement a practice management software suite.**
- **Put systems in place to manage finances, marketing, and patients.**
- **Hire an HR professional.**

Practice Management Software

Most dental businesses now run on some brand of practice management software. An office that's still operating without a computer system is probably very limited, with no more than two or three employees. The future for dentists is software, like it or not.

All recent graduates have exposure to technology like computer systems, digital X-rays, and Cerac, along with most of the newer technology. As you grow the size of your company, including specialties and locations, more complexities will appear. To build something that can grow, be insanely profitable, and sell for millions, you must digitize and centralize your data so that it can be analyzed and presented to management for review and decision-making.

Practice management suites differ from provider to provider, but most offer the same set of core features:

» Graphical patient oral charts
» A patient database
» An imaging database
» Instructional templates for common procedures
» Scheduling that coordinates patient, dentist, and hygienist schedules and automatically sends reminders and follow-up messages
» A patient portal that lets patients fill out their dental history, change their contact information, pay bills, and receive X-rays and other documents online
» Billing, insurance coding, and accounting
» Front-office features (patient check-in, check-out, daily to-do lists with reminders)

Your practice management system should also let you monitor your business metrics, including where patients are coming from and how much revenue each of your associates is producing. In other words, a good practice management system is an Entrepreneur Dentist's control center, dashboard, and decision-making "war room" all in one.

There are many such software suites on the market; some are stand-alone and others are enterprise systems. I personally used some form of Dentrix for most of my career, not necessarily because it was better than others, but because it was the most common. We had to spend less time training on it, because the people I hired had probably already used it. But there are many that my colleagues use:

- *CareStack* is highly recommended by many DSOs.
- *Open Dental* is open-source, which means there's no service behind it; but if you have an IT professional on your team, you can customize it to meet your specific needs. Most large DSOs that have their own IT departments will choose to build their own open-source platforms.
- *Dentrix* is owned by Henry Schein Inc., the company that controls the market for dental supplies. If you use their practice management software, integration with supply ordering will be smoother and easier.

But I suggest previewing multiple practice management solutions and finding the one that best suits your needs and budget.

LUCRATIVE LARRY'S ADVICE ON ... PRACTICE MANAGEMENT SYSTEMS

Locally hosted practice management software (the kind that you host on your servers in a server room) could cost $10,000 or more, depending

continued

on how many locations you have and the features you want. Cloud-based systems are sold by monthly subscription, and they typically cost around $199–$299 per month, with the cost going up as you grow. Up to a point, you can tie offices together with a remote access software like LogMeIn. But you will have to get an enterprise system to grow beyond a certain point. Pay the costs for a great tool and you'll get better results. Talk to an expert like NetFusion Consulting about making the right purchase, and be sure that whoever you trust can also provide your in-house staff with IT training. Implementing these new systems into your organization will require that someone on your staff have the training to understanding how to use technology to further your business goals.

Other Systems You Need

Of all the other systems you should have in place, start with a financial management and accounting system. Business is like playing a sport: You don't know how you're doing if you don't check the scoreboard. Your finances are your scoreboard. If you're not paying attention to the numbers, you might look at the books one day and wonder, "Why do I have no money? Why am I not ahead?"

Before I implemented a financial management system with Kids Dental Kare, when there were financial mix-ups, my CPA would blame my controller, my controller would blame the person who made the deposit, and I would get a report two or three months later. I couldn't make financial decisions based on something three months old.

When I finally got a system and a controller to run it, he could crunch numbers with spreadsheets and give me a fifty-day moving average on collections, revenues, and everything else. He could even show me debt servicing with visuals, so I could say, "Well, this will be paid off in X amount of time, and then my debt will be this." Your financial system should show you every facet of your financial life, including insurance reimbursements, collections information, and outstanding bills and their overdue status. You'll also have detailed records for your tax preparer, so you can avoid problems with Uncle Sam.

It's like sitting at the controls of your own financial aircraft carrier. Get financial software and hire or contract with someone who knows how to run it. Learn how to read a balance sheet. If you have something that crunches the numbers for you, you can fly by your instruments, and that's really how a business should operate.

A bit of advice—figure out how you'll deal with cash payments. Having cash in the office creates an unnecessary temptation for your staff, and that can't lead anywhere good. Have your financial person create a procedure for dealing with cash.

Here's why. Most dentists don't even realize how easy it is for staff to take the cash that patients use to pay, stick it in their pockets, and just not enter the payment on the books. Over the years, I had to devise an elaborate system of checking everybody in: Who was the patient; what procedure were they having done; were they an insurance or Medicare patient; and how were they paying? Because some patients still paid cash (which is a lot less common today, but still happens in some parts of the country), I had a drop box bolted to the wall.

The staff would collect the cash and drop it and a receipt into the drop box. To open it, the office manager had a key and I had a key. Both of us would have to open it together. It was like the procedure for launching missiles on a nuclear submarine. It was ridiculous, but it was necessary. Even then, people found a way to steal cash. The moral of the story is that if you have to do business in cash, make it temptation proof.

Real Estate and Facilities

Managing your real estate and marketing is less about software and more about people and processes. With real estate, if you have a broker who's helping you manage your leases and find new properties, he or she should also be able to set you up with a credible property manager. This person is responsible for the care and feeding of your physical locations—making sure maintenance is done, repairs are made, systems are operating normally, everything is up to code and in compliance with laws, and so on.

Marketing

You reap what you sow. So, sow well and in season, so you may reap well in harvest season. Marketing is the lifeblood of every business, because without new customers, all business will eventually fail. That's why we say, "Marketing is everything we do." But you know that doesn't necessarily translate to your new hires. I've worked on a lot of systems to try to build a happy, welcoming office environment, but you have to hire people who are happy, stable, and disciplined in order to see that.

The challenge is that even the best screening will miss things about people when you hire them. You must have a system of evaluating hires early and often, with clear documentation, in case you need to discipline or terminate them. However, when your messages are congruent and all your team members and assets are in alignment, that's when you will get the greatest *leverage*.

Leverage is a term that banks use to communicate their debt-to-equity ratio. But I use it as a way of thinking about force: A lever delivers a force that can move things of great weight, and I want to use that force to move people and markets for my benefit. That's what DSOs do. They leverage economies of scale, vendor relations, management, legal expertise, and finances. At higher levels, the spending is more targeted and organized, with more access to capital and strategic planning.

You may not be able to exert much leverage now, but as you grow, you will. For example, I already mentioned how difficult it can be to get some associate dentists to cooperate with an office experience script and culture. Well, as you grow, you gain more leverage over those dentists because you have more to offer. *Higher pay? Sure, I can offer that. Equity? We can discuss it. Assistance with starting your own office? Certainly. However, I need you to be 100 percent on board with my patient experience plan. That's a deal breaker.* When you have a lot to offer, you have power. That's leverage.

I've already discussed tracking all marketing spending and logging every patient interaction, click-through, and opened email to see what's working and what's not. Beyond that, it's smart to keep a database of vendors—printers, designers, and the like—so you're not searching for people when you need them most. Also, have your collateral materials, and every other printed piece you use, on a drive, updated and ready to send to a printer at the click of a mouse. You can stop advertising, but you can never stop marketing.

Also, keep lots of arrows in your quiver and keep multiple campaigns going. Never be dependent on one source of new customers, because if that source goes belly-up, so will your cash flow.

Human Resources

This can be a minefield, so my advice is straightforward: Do *not* do HR yourself. Hire someone or contract with an outside HR agency to handle all personnel matters. You need to be sure you're following all the labor laws, handling associate pay in a way that's fair and won't cause conflict, and avoiding legal pitfalls when you have to let someone go.

I share my own horror story as an example of what not to do. I hired a woman who had her HR certification to manage personnel for me, and we had a dental assistant who had been absent from work off and on. She'd be tardy. She wouldn't show up. There was a report that she was using drugs. I hadn't fired her yet, but then she didn't show up three days in a row, and my HR person said, "She's been here less than a year, Dr. Lanier. You can terminate her without consequences."

Well, she was wrong. I fired the woman, and she took me to court for wrongful termination. It turned out that she'd been pregnant and having personal problems, and that was a valid excuse for her absences. That whole fiasco cost me $130,000, not including attorneys' fees. That was the cost of my HR person's bad advice.

After that, I purchased employee insurance, which is basically a team of labor attorneys that you have to consult when you do anything involving one of your people—even if you're going to write somebody up. It was a safety net, and I hated it because I had to go through all sorts of extra steps to do anything. But it prevented me from going over that ledge again. My system became "Do not discipline anyone until you've bounced it off the lawyers, and copy me, copy operations, and send it to risk management. They'll tell us what we can do." We would not move on anything related to HR until the lawyers gave us the green light.

That's part of success. As you grow, things will get a lot more complex. Do yourself a favor and find a reputable agency or an experienced HR manager to handle things.

TALK TO THE EXPERT

Our philosophy is that too many people want strategies and tactics, but they don't work on their own leadership ability or on getting the right team around them. The common denominator around the effective group or single practice is that they have a great CEO and a fantastic leadership team. These are some of the top leadership training options:

» Dental Success Institute with Dr. Mark Costes

» Breakaway Seminars by Dr. Scott Leune, ideal for newer dentist-entrepreneurs

» ADSO.org, for very large organizations

» Dentist Entrepreneur Organization, led by Jacob Puhl

There are also four dental conferences that are musts: the ADSO annual conference; the Henry Schein Dental Annual National Sales Meeting; the DEO Summit; and the Dykema annual conference.

—Darin Acopan, Vice President of Business Development for the DEO[21]

KEEP IN MIND

» **You have to assume risk and manage it.**

» **The "time off" test takes inhuman discipline.**

» **The better your system, the higher your multiple.**

21 Telephone interview, October 1, 2018.

Risk Management

Your HR attorneys can function as a risk management department as your franchise grows, both protecting you against risks that are already in place and educating your people in avoiding potential future risks. That will become a bigger deal as you get deeper pockets.

Years ago, I had a specialist on my staff who refused to treat a child with HIV. I don't know what was on her mind, but she told the mom, "You could bring her back when everybody else is gone." The parent was angry and humiliated, but she also knew that we couldn't discriminate like that, and the you-know-what hit the fan.

Even the judge said, "There's something wrong here. You have Dr. Lanier here, and I'm sure he's the one with deep pockets. You don't even have the doctor who did it." The parent sued me, I wound up settling, and it cost me another $60,000–$70,000. After that (again, closing the barn door after the horse tramples everything), I put clauses in my associate employment agreement that the dentists had certain responsibilities and liabilities. That's risk management.

Here's something else that will happen as you become successful: Another Entrepreneur Dentist will come and work for you to steal some of your ideas. You can tell when this is happening, because the doctor will constantly be asking, "How do you do that? What software did you use for this?" If they're taking notes and walking around, they're not going to be there that long, and they might try to steal some of your staff when they leave. But that's part of the process. Everybody steals something from somebody. That's how the game is played. Try to bake that into the cake and just decide to stay out in front of your competitors. All great games are competitive, especially when it comes to making money.

Can You Take Time Off?

If you build a robust system with strong training and documentation, you might believe you can take a month off and things will keep humming. But that takes extraordinary discipline, and most practices don't have that. Use the "time off test" as a gauge of how well you're doing at making your dental business systematic.

Take a few days off and see how things run. If things don't fall apart, take a week off. Then two weeks. Keep going until you can take a month off and not lose money. If you've built that kind of system, you've built a saleable business. Be ready to hand over the reins to someone else when you go into the final year of your exit strategy, because you'll be working with the exit team every day, with little time left to run the company. The more organized and prepared you are on the way to your exit, the easier and less time-consuming it will be. Plus, buyers love to see a business that runs smoothly without the founder at the helm.

Trust your system. If you put a system in place and you implement it, you'll get results as good as the system you're following. Dentists who don't have a system end up working for the ones who do. With the right system, your business becomes more efficient, and efficiency builds your multiple, because your business is more profitable.

EYEING THE EXIT

The point of a comprehensive system is to make you, the dentist-owner, obsolete. Your business will be more attractive to buyers if they don't need to keep you on to make sure things run smoothly.

If you have documented procedures, a practice management system,

continued

and a strong management team under you, buyers will know they can come in and effect a seamless transition without having you stay around until a management team is trained. That's better for you, because your business is more valuable and should fetch a higher price. It also makes it less likely that you will be asked to stay on as one of the conditions of the sale, which can and does happen. If you'd like to be free to enjoy your wealth after selling, put a system in place.

CHAPTER 6

Build Your Team

CHECK YOUR GPS

It's time to make the transition from dental practice to business, which is all about putting systems in place.

- » **Deliberately define your destination**: What systems would you like to put in place in the next year? Financial? HR? Marketing?
- » **Lock it into your internal GPS**: The people who will help you implement those systems are a system themselves. Your office manager, practice manager, staff—they all need to be trained on your systems and procedures.
- » **Choose an ETA**: Choose a goal date when you'll try the "time off test" and check how well things run in your absence.
- » **Devise your plan**: Begin documenting every activity that occurs in your office, from patient interactions to ordering supplies.
- » **Get started now**: Start shopping for practice management software suites. If you don't have an IT pro on staff or a consultant under contract, get someone before you shop.
- » **Trust the plan and keep moving.**

I'm a spiritual man, so it pains me to say this, but it's true: Some people are just not good people. But you need good people; you can't build even a single office without them. However, you have *got* to watch your back and not be too trusting, or some folks will take advantage of you and leave you standing there, shocked and hurt. Good people are hard to find.

Case in point—when I had my small office in Hammond, Louisiana, with only a few patients, I hired a girl to come in and run my QuickBooks. Well, the girl opened a bank account with her cousin, then started forging my signature on checks and depositing money in her account. At one point, I was waiting on an insurance check that never came. I called the insurance company and they said, "You cashed the check." I assured them that I hadn't, so they sent me a copy of the canceled check. There was the evidence, in my hand, with my phony signature on it. I felt disgusted. When I confronted the girl about what she had done, her defense for embezzlement was "Doc, I needed it more than you."

I wish that was the only time such a thing happened, but it's not. When I started Kids Dental Kare, I hired another woman to handle billing and accounting. I should have known something was up, because after a while, when I came up front, she was secretive. She'd say, "Doc, you hired me to do this. Can I do my work and you do yours?" That should have been a red flag, because it was my practice and my business, and I had a right to know *everything* she was doing on my dime—but I didn't press it. When you're honest, you want to believe that other people are honest, too, and that's not always the case.

After a while, the bank called me to ask if I'd opened a joint account, because this woman had deposited $10,000 in the account. That was just one check; God knows how much cash she had taken me for before I fired her.

THINK:

- **Being the boss means not trusting people until they prove themselves.**
- **When you find people you can trust, hold on to them.**

Transitioning from Dentist to Boss

I wish I could say those were the only times people stole from me, but I can't. The lesson here is that at some point, if you aspire to build a business that will make you rich, you will have to make that mental transition from the friendly dentist who trusts everybody to the boss who trusts nobody.

I'm not saying that no one can be trusted. I am saying that just as you put systems in place to run your business, you have to put a new approach to personnel in place to build that business. That approach has to be built on the idea of "trust but verify." Hire the best people you can, but do not assume they are competent or trustworthy until they prove it. Trust is earned. Until the people you hire earn your trust, have systems in place to monitor what they do, make sure they're accountable for doing their work, and put checks in place to make it hard for them to damage your business—like my two-key drop box bolted to the wall.

Some workers might see something like that as an insult, an admission that you don't trust them. That's naïve. It's an admission of reality. *Do not* apologize for protecting your business and your future. As the Bob Sugar character said in the movie *Jerry Maguire*, "It's not show friends, it's show business."

I owe a big debt of thanks to my former operations manager, Theresa, for keeping me out of trouble with hiring. She became my confidante and advisor; she and my wife would advise me about people they thought were bad news. When some new hire would come in and give Theresa a bad vibe, she would take me aside and say, "Doc, watch her." She was usually right. She was protecting me. It's good to have people like that, and she did a really good job. Thank you, Theresa.

By the way, not everyone is untrustworthy. When you keep an eye on your employees and hold them accountable, the lazy or dishonest ones will leave (or you'll have to terminate them, because letting them stay is bad for morale). But the good ones will stay. Those are the people to build around. When you do find good people you can trust, keep them.

DO

- **Again, work with an HR professional.**
- **Other dentists will make or break your business.**
- **After associate dentists, your office manager will make or break you.**

Hiring Doctors

Before I get into how crucial it is to be smart and careful when you're hiring other dentists, let me reiterate one point from the last chapter: *Work with an HR professional in all of what I'm about to tell you.* Seriously. Do not wade into the waters of hiring and firing people without professional assistance or you'll drown. For good information on where to start, try the Society for Human Resource Management at www.shrm.org.

It's not overselling to say that the associate dentists you hire will make or break your dental business. After you, they are the primary representatives of your brand, and when your business gets big enough that you're no longer spending a lot of time chairside, they become brand *custodians.* Finding skilled associates who are good with patients and who will be assets to your business is never easy, but don't skimp. A bad doctor can damage your brand and cost you dearly.

Here's one example. At one point, I had a hard time recruiting associate dentists. Sometimes, the people just aren't there. You run an ad but you're not getting responses. I needed someone and finally hired this young doctor, but immediately his work became suspect; it didn't look right. Before you knew it, Denti-Cal was investigating the cases and pulling all the charts of the patients he had worked on. I didn't do any of the work, but since I was the owner/doctor, I was responsible. I ended up on the Denti-Cal watch list and it slowed business down for everybody. Worse, I didn't have anybody to replace him, and we had patients, so I had to let him stay until I found somebody. It would have been better to close the office temporarily—anything but letting that bad work go out my door. That one guy hurt me.

I hired another guy who did good clinical work and was very productive, but he wouldn't communicate with the parents or the children. He was brusque and rough with patients. I kept him as long as I could, but he was so arrogant that he was bad for my brand and for office morale. When he asked me, "Should I remind you how much I produced last year?" he was done. For these liability reasons, many DSOs consider branding each office differently and using different corporations for each location (Dr. X, Dr. Y, etc.). It's not a bad idea when you have a doc who's a skilled practitioner but you worry he or she might be a loose cannon.

When you hire associates, have a clear, objective evaluation process. For example, after the disaster with the new doctor, we created a review process for new associates. We would take pre-op and post-op X-rays, have the manager upload them, and I could review them from home and take some decisive action if it was needed.

I also started writing evaluations of my associates, and the word I started using when things weren't right was "unacceptable." If I had to write a doctor up, I would describe the work as unacceptable. As in, "Steve, what you're giving me is unacceptable. We need things to change." I started giving associates plenty of warning if their work wasn't up to par. If they wouldn't comply and make some changes, we would cut down their days from five to maybe three. If an associate only gets paid based on patient collections, and they're not in the office, they're not earning a living.

If Theresa, my office manager, took a dentist down from five days to three, they'd always call me and ask why. I'd say, "Here's the reason. We had some 'unacceptables.' Let's see if we can get back to what's acceptable, and then, maybe, you can get some days back." Then it's up to them to change. If they can't change, then eventually you have to cut bait.

The reality is that good young dentists are always going to be in high demand, and sometimes the best you can do is make your expectations clear to them, then pull the trigger—let them come in and show you what they can do.

Here are some of the best practices I learned, usually the hard way, for hiring dentists who can be assets to your business:

- ***Know when you really need someone.*** There's nothing worse than hiring an associate and learning that he or she is a cash drain, not a profit center. A solid rule of thumb for a general dental practice needing an associate is—
  - At least 2,000 active patients
  - Patient bookings at least two months out
  - Cash reserves to cover up to one year of an associate's salary before he or she becomes profitable

» ***Know what you need.*** Having too many patients for your current roster of dentists is a nice problem, but that's not the only reason to bring in an associate. Maybe there are procedures that you're not great at but would like to provide. Maybe you've been referring out a lot of work in areas like endodontics or cosmetics and would love to keep that revenue in-house. Maybe there's a service not being offered in your market. Rather than just hiring a warm body, figure out how much revenue you could bring in by offering additional services or by servicing more general patients. If the numbers work out, hire someone—always keeping in mind that when you factor in salary, benefits, and overhead, it still takes a while for a new dentist to become cash flow positive.

» ***Enforce a probationary period.*** All kinds of things can go wrong with a new hire in any industry, and dentistry is no exception. Your new associate could be lazy, have a bad chairside manner, clash with the staff, or any other number of warts that you won't see until after they're on board. I strongly recommend having a mandatory trial period of (usually) ninety days, so you can make sure everything works out before you enter into a long-term relationship with a new doctor.

» ***Be crystal clear on your relationship and the dentist's position.*** Is your new associate going to be a full-time employee, an independent contractor, or a buy-in partner who will help you grow the practice? Each has its advantages and disadvantages. Full-time employment works well for recent dental school graduates and inexperienced doctors, while doctors with established reputations might prefer the flexibility of contractor status. Be sure you firmly establish your associate's status, duties, responsibilities, and compensation package (collections, guaranteed salary, bonuses, etc.). Also establish terms for renewing, renegotiating, or terminating your employment contract (for instance, a mutual option after a certain amount of time), as well as the terms of the associate's resignation, such as sixty days' written notice.

» ***Help your associates grow.*** Your associates are just as aware of the income potential of dentistry as you are, so many of them will probably aspire to have their own practices. In that case, you have two choices: Watch them leave or help them grow. That's one of the things that I could have done better. I lost a lot of doctors who became my competitors because I did not offer them enough opportunities to start an office under their own name. If I had done that, we could have kept it under my brand, and my business would have been that much bigger.

If an associate proves to be skilled, trustworthy, and able to manage people, consider giving them some ownership of one of your locations. Limit what that dentist is responsible for so that you can help them succeed. For example, they accept responsibility for the administration and day-to-day operations of the office, but your company still handles marketing, financials, and all the rest. For the right person, this can powerfully incentivize them to become more productive for you.

DSOs do this sort of thing frequently. By giving individual dentists the chance to launch offices under their own name, they not only reward great entrepreneurs but also build a firewall between each practice, as we discussed earlier. If Dr. Smith runs his five offices into a ditch, that doesn't impact Dr. Jones, Dr. Ramirez, or any of the DSO's 400 other locations.

» ***Protect yourself.*** This goes back to hiring an HR professional who can handle all these agreements, contracts, and everything else for you—

but it doesn't stop there. It's also important to include non-compete and non-solicitation language in your associate employment agreements. Now, some states don't allow non-competes, but your HR pro will know that. You're trying to ensure that if your associate decides to leave, he or she isn't trying to steal your patients, damaging your reputation in the process.

In general, bringing in a new associate is about adapting, setting clear expectations, and providing opportunities for growth. Make sure the front office staff touts a new associate as being a highly skilled professional, just like you. Make each new associate feel welcome. Explain procedures and company culture. Let associates know how they're performing according to objective metrics: number of patients, revenue, and feedback. Evaluate new docs for personality, compatibility with your practice, and skills and productivity, and give it time. No new associate is going to be a profit machine overnight.

LUCRATIVE LARRY'S ADVICE ON . . . PRACTICE MANAGERS

What should you pay a practice manager? That's like asking what you should pay for a heart transplant. You need both to survive. My bottom line is that if a practice manager is good and comes with fantastic references, he or she is worth it. Check out the person thoroughly, but when you find someone great, pay whatever they're worth.

Hire Great Practice Managers

Associate dentists are your most critical people, but losing anyone hurts your practice. According to research by the Society for Human Resource Management, when a business of any kind has to replace a salaried employee, the process generally costs an amount equal to six to nine months of that person's salary.[22] Darin Acopan of the DEO says, "Everyone is focused on saving costs in labs and supplies, which is only five to seven percent of the pie. You can only squeeze so much juice out of that. They don't focus on the costs of patient attrition or of members leaving."[23]

Out of all the people who can leave your practice, none will hurt you more than a good practice manager walking out. Practice managers run every aspect of the day-to-day operations of your office (and sometimes, multiple offices):

» Ensuring your offices are in compliance with everything from health codes to safety and labor laws
» Auditing finances and dentist performance
» Managing patient scheduling systems
» Managing associate and staff scheduling
» Reviewing patient payment activity and collections
» Ordering supplies
» Managing payroll, personnel files, and training
» Managing marketing and advertising activities
» Issuing reports for you, the dentist-owner

In other words, your practice manager is your invaluable right hand, the

---

22 Julie Silard Kantor, "High Turnover Costs Way More Than You Think," *HuffPost,* February 11, 2017, www.huffingtonpost.com/julie-kantor/high-turnover-costs-way-more-than-you-think_b_9197238.html.

23 Telephone interview, October 1, 2018.

individual probably most responsible for transitioning your dental practice into a franchise-able business. Your practice manager will have his or her (most are women) fingerprints on every operational aspect of your company, from insurance to contracts to records to marketing. They are also the person who will make it possible for you to step away from chairside at your home location and focus more on growing your business.

When Kids Dental Kare started growing, I was at one or more of my offices from eight in the morning to eight at night, six days a week. Not only is that not sustainable, it's micromanaging. I was attending to things I didn't need to be attending to—associate performance, patient service, and finances—when I should have been recruiting top associates, finding great new locations, locking down financing for expansion, and connecting with people in the community. Hiring Theresa, my amazing practice manager, relieved me of that. A great practice manager frees you to act more like a CEO.

A practice manager is literally an executive, because she has to be able to execute—to get things done efficiently, enforce the dentist-owner's wishes, lead a team, and keep multiple balls in the air without dropping any of them. Theresa happened to be really good at it because her husband is a dentist. For some reason, she enjoyed going through all the training seminars that dental practice managers have available to them. Because we dealt so often with Medicaid, she went to all of the Medicaid seminars and became an expert in it. Everyone respected her, and she became like everybody's mom.

If you have someone within your office who has the organizational, communication, and leadership skills to potentially be a great practice manager, your best bet might be to get her some training and then promote from within. Your operations manager needs to have (preferably) a college education and a great work ethic—in addition to experience in dentistry, billing, accounting, and a broad range of management skills. Even then, you have to spend money on professional development and enable them to take plenty of courses to grow with the company. This is one reason you want to hold on to this person for a long time. You have to invest training, time, money, and trust in her, and you don't want someone coming along and stealing your investment.

Other Key Members of Your Team

Your practice manager is the linchpin of your growing business, but you'll need other people on the team if you're going to build something of value that you can sell for a lot of money. The first is an executive, probably a controller. At the later stages, you'll want a chief operating officer (COO), but be careful not to hand that title out too quickly to someone not qualified. We chose to stick with a controller and a CPA and to outsource the role of CFO, as needed, to an outside expert with experience in mergers and acquisitions, so that he could guide us through the final stages of the exit.

If I had known years ago what I know now, I would have started with my exit in mind and reverse-engineered everything. I would have worked with my controller and CPA to create my financial system and hired a CFO biannually, to review, advise, and consult. That would have allowed for a more efficient process as we grew and moved toward a sale.

If you're running more than three locations, and you won't, or can't, step away from chairside to focus on running and growing the business, consider bringing on someone who will function as a COO. This isn't easy, because you have to let go of some of your control. But a COO isn't a dentist, which means you can stay chairside and do what you do best while he's busy recruiting practice managers and other key personnel, lining up funding sources, taking care of any legal matters, and attending to other mission-critical items that might otherwise slip through the cracks.

A full-time COO is expensive and might also ask for equity in your practice, so a better option for many dentist-owners is a *fractional* COO. That means the COO is a contractor who invests X hours per week in your business and works a part-time schedule. Still, many fractional COOs are retired from the corporate world and have vast amounts of knowledge and experience. If you're running something small, with just six to ten locations, that's probably just the ticket for you.

Even if you can't hire a COO (and even if you can), strongly consider hiring a fractional CFO. I hired Scott when I realized that having clean books and financial records was vital to my goal of selling Kids Dental Kare for a lot of money. You'll already have a controller or bookkeeper, and you should definitely have a relationship with a CPA who follows generally accepted accounting principles (GAAP), but your CFO will be the expert who advises and checks up on their work. A good CFO will be worth the $30,000–$40,000 you'll pay them, because they'll see things you won't.

A CFO is crucial because as you get larger, your reporting requirements get stricter. Also, when you go to lenders for the money to open four new locations in a year, they're going to subject your business to a level of scrutiny that you're not prepared for. Your CFO will make sure you're prepared, so that potential investors, lenders, the IRS, or anyone else can look at your books and say, "This practice is on the right track." Your CFO will also be the one who tells you how to optimize your company to be as appealing as possible when you sell.

This is important in dentistry because it's not uncommon for even multi-office practices to still be handling their finances the way they did when it was just the one dentist and a receptionist. I've been shocked to find practices that are turning $10 million in revenue but are still doing everything from a shoebox. That's *dangerous*.

Here's an example of how dangerous. One of my cousins had a construction business and was having some health problems. He called me and said he needed to borrow $150,000, and my heart went out to him. I was prepared to lend him the money, but then I talked to one of our mutual childhood friends who's a CPA. He said, "Be careful. He's generating a lot of money, but he's still got his little sister doing the books, and she never took an accounting class." Apparently, my cousin had no idea how much cash or debt he had. That's scary, because eventually that catches up with you in a big way.

In the end, the risk was too great for me. I didn't lend him the money. I knew it would only be throwing money down a hole. Well, that's how lending institutions will look at you. Are you sophisticated enough to lend to, or will lending you money be throwing it down a hole? Your financials will tell the story, because banks know numbers. You, as the dentist-owner, might not be sophisticated at finance, but you need someone who is. There are resource companies that hire out fractional CFOs to dental businesses, or you can look at an organization like the ADSO or DEO. But once you get past three locations, you should hire someone.

The other professional you simply cannot survive without is your attorney. I probably gave away a few million in my final exit from Kids Dental Kare because I failed to get good legal counsel. As you grow, you will become a target for everyone, from unscrupulous associates who want to copy your business model to competitors who will claim that you stole *their* business model. Find a law firm that has experience working with dental practices and pay them what you need to.

You might need legal counsel for any number of reasons, but there are three main areas of law that are relevant to a dental business, and your firm should have attorneys experienced in all of them:

» **Liability**—Anytime you're dealing with medical treatment, there will be accusations of unsanitary conditions, patients who don't like their veneers, and flat-out shady claims. You need liability insurance, but you also need a good litigator to protect you.

» **Trademarks**—When I finally came up with my Kids Dental Kare logo, I had a trademark and patent attorney trademark my name and logo right away. Plan on doing that if you intend to grow, because shady dentists will pirate your name and logo as quickly as Chinese manufacturers knock off Louis Vuitton handbags.

» **Taxes**—The penalties for unpaid payroll taxes can be ruinous, so don't risk falling behind. Have an attorney experienced in taxation for small businesses and run everything by them before you close out your books.

My blanket advice on lawyers is to hire good ones and then use them. Don't make a move without them, even if you think you know what you're doing. You know dentistry; they know law, finance, and how the courts work. A good law firm will protect you if you let it. But attorneys and CPAs, or anyone that gets paid on billable hours, should be watched closely for results: Lawyers don't get paid to start fights, but to keep them going.

Any billable-hours associate automatically has a conflict of interest with me. I'm trying to pay as little as I can, and they are trying to charge me as much as they can. Keep things tight with your lawyer. Don't have the "How's the family?" conversation, because when you check your billing statement, you'll find out that most of them are charging you while they laugh along with or at you. Keep all conversations strictly business.

That's not the end of the list of people you need, either. Your CFO will be most effective if you're working with a CPA who handles all your bookkeeping and tax records. Again, there are companies you can contract with for a CPA/controller, or you can hire someone through an organization like the Dental Accounting Association, a network of CPA firms that works to improve dental practice accounting, tax planning, and profit coaching. But in either case, no shoeboxes allowed—no QuickBooks, either. That's fine for a single office, but you need more powerful bookkeeping software as you grow, and you can usually find it in practice management suites like the ones I discussed earlier.

A great CPA will work with your CFO to make sure your entire business is in compliance with tax and reporting laws and give you the cleanest possible financials, which will come in handy when you're trying to get a loan or sitting down across from a private equity firm that wants to buy what you've built.

You'll also want a good IT manager, because between front and back office practice management systems and your website, today's practices *run* on technology. You probably won't need this person full-time, but I suggest contracting with a company that has a strong track record for reliability and uptime. Your IT management contractor will need to ensure that your internal network stays up and running, files are backed up and secure, any servers you operate are updated with the newest software, your Internet connectivity is fast and dependable, your website is always open for business, and you have backups to keep your business running if computers crash—or the Internet in your area goes dark.

Finally, make friends with a smart lender. As your offices continue to generate revenue and you eye further growth, you will need the advice of someone who can help you finance your expansion. This has become especially challenging since the recession that began in 2008. There's lingering fear and uncertainty in the financial sector because of the losses that hit dental practices, as well as everyone else, so once you get past three or four locations and need more than about $5 million in capital, regular banks will usually not lend to you, even with the great track record that dentists have. You need to find other ways to scale.

It hasn't always been this way. When I started, it was on the heels of the savings and loan debacle of the 1990s, and money was expensive. Now, it's very cheap. That's led dentists who aren't ready to expand to *think* they're ready; and lenders are skeptical of any dentist who wants to grow but lacks the experience and infrastructure. Once you've established that you are doing well, and they see that you're generating a lot of cash, you'll have an easier time. Until then, it's good to have a banker by your side to walk you through the requirements and obligations.

TALK TO THE EXPERT

It's important for Entrepreneur Dentists to appreciate how risk plays a significant role in a business exit strategy. Whether you are selling to an associate dentist, creating a strategic partnership with a competitor, or "taking chips off the table" by selling a majority ownership interest to a capital equity sponsor group, the level of business risk associated with a sale transaction can greatly impact the value of the business.

Early on when building the business, Entrepreneur Dentists often ignore risks or bend rules to maximize current profits. What's more problematic is when these owners move forward on significant operational initiatives or contractual transactions without expertise. This lack of knowledge often has unintended consequences and can subject the business to various risks. Whether it's establishing proper human resource policies, negotiating payer contracts, entering into contractual agreements, understanding regulatory requirements, or determining practice location

continued

profitability, it is imperative to bring in the right HR, operational, legal, and CPA/CFO personnel to ensure a tolerable level of risk. This will also help the business grow strategically and achieve maximum profitability.

When it's time to sell the business, the right support team will also help obtain a higher purchase price. Take the need for proper accounting as an example. It's possible to look at a bank account for the year and say, "This was the total of deposits and checks issued. Therefore, net cash generated for the year is the cash profit, and so the practice is worth this much." That may work for a small single practice, but for a multi-site practice with several lines of specialties, that level of accounting detail would not be acceptable to sophisticated investors. Such investors expect profitability and cash flow analysis by month, office, provider, patient mix, payer, etc. Accordingly, it's important to bring in a CFO/controller with the proper expertise to build a solid financial system that can be used to effectively manage the business and, at the same time, is flexible enough to expand as the business grows.

Financial information is also used extensively for profitability analysis and financial projections, and thus heavily scrutinized during the buyer's due diligence process. As a buyer gets more comfortable with the accuracy and reliability of the seller's financials, the risk of making an offer is significantly lower. This increased level of assurance in the financial numbers reduces the risk that a buyer will negotiate down the purchase price or walk away from the transaction altogether due to financial uncertainties.

Reduce risk and maximize your investment: Get the right professionals and advisors involved early on to help you grow and manage the business. Don't wait until it's too late in the game to prepare to sell your business.

—Scott Patterson, Partner, Hardesty LLC[24]

24 Email interview, October 10, 2018.

KEEP IN MIND

- **DIY any of this only as long as you have to.**
- **Don't let people become entitled.**
- **Listen to your experts.**

Do It Yourself . . . If You Have To

Every one of these people, even the contractors and fractional executives, costs big money. That's why in the beginning, if you're one dentist running a single office, you may have to DIY some of this stuff. I know I said not to, but early on, you'll have no choice. While you're small, you can probably get by handling HR decisions and practice management yourself. But as soon as you're ready to open a second office, you're officially too big for DIY personnel and practice management. Hire someone.

No matter what, never open your doors, even to a single office, without legal and financial experts on your team. The potential damage for a bad decision or an oversight is simply too great.

It's also important to be careful not to let your key people become entitled enough to think that they, not you, are in charge. I've seen this happen. Practice managers, or even associate dentists, given a lot of power to run things, think they can run them *their* way instead of *your* way. That's why it's important to keep a little bit of distance between you and them to remind them that you are still the boss.

This is where great practice managers can be both a blessing and a curse. Near the end, I had some offices that I would only visit every two or three months, because they were doing extremely well without me ever visiting. The manager was doing something right, because they were the most efficient and productive offices I had. However, the trouble with one of those offices was that the doctors and staff had become a clique. I was an outsider—me, the guy who was paying all the bills—and I couldn't penetrate the clique.

If that happens to you, and you send somebody else in to try to change things, they're going to be persecuted. There's this sense that "We're not going to conform to what you say." And while you could say "Oh yes you are" and fire everybody, you're just sabotaging yourself, because you just tore down a profitable office. You just have to keep pushing until you can change the culture, which takes time.

Be on the lookout for that sort of entitled attitude. I've had managers talk about "My crew and my staff," and I have to remind them, "Listen, everything there is mine. It's not your crew. It's *my* crew. And you work for me as well. So, let's get that straight." That's not pleasant, but it is necessary. Sometimes, you have to remind people who's in charge.

Good people will want autonomy, and you'll need to give it to them, within reason. But you also need to let them know that you have well-documented policies and procedures that you follow, and following them is *not* optional. Anyone who can't do that has to go, because you can't have people making policy from the bottom up.

Two final pieces of advice. First, listen to your legal, financial, HR, tech, and marketing experts, especially when they're telling you what you don't want to hear. Second, join the Association of Dental Support Organizations (ADSO): It's a group of owners of DSOs. I joined—and it was expensive—but it was a fantastic resource. You'll be able to pick the brains of the CEOs and managers of some of the largest DSOs in America, and that's where you'll find the solutions to a lot of your challenges.

EYEING THE EXIT

When you start to look at a possible exit, you'll need to make sure that you've switched your bookkeeping from cash accounting to accrual accounting. In cash accounting, you record revenue when it's received; in accrual accounting, you record revenue when you earn it, such as when patients are billed.

There are two big reasons to make the switch. First, the IRS will only allow businesses doing less than $5 million in revenue to use cash accounting, so using accrual will prevent tax issues. Second, any potential buyer will want to audit your books, and this can only be done accurately if they were compiled using accrual accounting. Save yourself the downstream hassles: If you're running more than two offices, switch to accrual now.

CHAPTER 7

Do Good Work and Follow the Plan

CHECK YOUR GPS

Let's assume for the purposes of this chapter that you're running two offices, and both are making money. You're starting to see the potential to build something that could change your life. Now what?

» **Deliberately define your destination**: Who do you need on your team to go from a dentist's office to a business?

» **Lock it into your internal GPS**: Determine how you will find those crucial experts: CFO, CPA, HR manager, practice manager, and law firm. List professional organizations, dentistry organizations, and referral sources that you could recruit from.

» **Choose an ETA**: When do you intend to have your key people in place?

» **Devise your plan**: When you have them in place, how will that change what you do? Where will you allocate your time and energy?

» **Get started now**: Start sending out inquiries about key

continued

personnel to those you know in the dental industry. If you can, start scheduling interviews.

- **Trust the plan and keep moving.**

We're in the final third of the book, and at this point, I hope you have some of the basics of building a multimillion-dollar dental business locked into your mind: building a great team, determining your niche, implementing a strong marketing plan, and so on. At this point, there's one other step I want you to take before you really dig into the work of building something: *Educate yourself.*

I took business classes to learn the essentials. I learned how to read financial statements and deal with business taxes—that sort of thing. But there's a lot more to know, and the more you learn now, the smoother things will go for you in the future. Learn what lawyers do in a business context. Learn what a CPA does in a business context. Learn the basics of information technology and what it does for your business. You're going to be hiring people to provide services for you, and ignorance leads to hiring the wrong people.

Even a basic accounting or business class, something you attend two days a week at five o'clock, after your clinical work is done, can make a huge difference. You don't need an MBA—you've already spent plenty of time in school becoming a dentist—but even a rudimentary education will help you ask better questions and avoid mistakes, as well as give you a leg up on your competition.

THINK

- **There are three paths to growth in dentistry.**
- **When you have two offices, you're prototyping.**
- **Now is the time to test all your procedures.**

Two Offices—What's Next?

Let's say that at this point, you're running two locations. You're pulling in close to $2 million in revenue from them, but you're also working six days a week, about twelve hours a day, and you're getting stretched pretty thin. At the same time, you can see the potential in this. You can see a time, in five years, when you might have six or eight offices and be on your way to building something pretty valuable. But obviously, you can't build it by doing what you've been doing.

You need a plan.

First, a disclaimer—your path might not be my path. My goal with this book is to teach you to think like an entrepreneur and give you the tools to succeed, but that doesn't mean your version of success has to look like mine. I chose to build something and sell it; you might have a different future in mind. In dentistry, there are basically three paths you can follow:

1. Grow a dental group and sell it to investors.
2. Grow it and partner with a larger group.
3. Grow it on your own to a size to be determined.

I chose the first one, and this book is written with that objective in mind. But depending on the direction you choose, you're going to build a different infrastructure. What I'm doing here is laying out the foundational pieces of that infrastructure based on my own experience. Later on, when you're working directly with a mentor, you can make adjustments to fit your personal goals. Remember, dental is not like medical; there is no liquidity event playbook. It's something of a minefield, and the way you get through a minefield is to follow in the footsteps of the people who passed through it before you.

Okay, moving on. Your plan should consist of the following components:

- Tested, documented processes and procedures for everything
- Rock-solid practice management software
- A vetted and compliant financial management system
- An office "playbook" that makes it easy to standardize everything at all your locations
- A comprehensive marketing plan with ROI tracking
- A regular schedule for real estate/new location scouting
- Your team in place: practice manager, HR professional, CFO, and lawyer

Working on all of this gives you your best opportunity to build a prototype of your perfect office. Right now, the stakes are relatively low. You don't have a lot of employees, you're probably not carrying a big bank loan, and because revenues haven't taken off yet, if there are IRS penalties for messing up the books, they will be relatively minor. This is the time to figure out the bugs in your system. Try everything, test everything, and see what works in your original location. When systems or processes work, see if you can replicate them in your second location. If you can, then you have a formula.

That's the technical name for franchises in industries like fast food, by the way: *formula businesses*. Go see the movie *The Founder* and watch how Ray Kroc took the standardized, tested methods of the McDonald brothers, which changed the way people made, bought, and ate hamburgers, and packaged them so that they could be replicated by anyone, anywhere in the world. You're not looking to serve ninety-nine billion burgers, but you want that kind of repeatable efficiency and excellence. That's what's going to get you to twenty locations, $20 million in revenue, and the lifestyle you want.

Documentation Flow

This is the time to create a business "playbook" that documents every facet of everything you do on a daily basis in your office: what happens when patients arrive and check in; what happens while they're in the waiting area; what happens chairside; what happens after the procedure; what happens at check-out; when subsequent appointments are set; how you ask for referrals and reviews; how you handle complaints; how you hire; how you fire; how supplies get ordered; your vendors for printing, design, social media, and cleaning and disinfecting clinical spaces; the office décor . . . everything.

The best way to deal with this is to walk through a typical week at your office with your practice manager. Go from turning on the lights on Monday to shutting things down on Friday—or Saturday, if you're open Saturdays. Take nothing for granted; break down everything, looking to optimize efficiency, productivity, cost savings, and patient experience. Ask tons of questions:

» Should we place referral materials in the waiting areas where patients might take them?

» Do we need more handicapped parking spaces or better parking lot lighting?

» Are we getting a fair price for cleaning services?

» Do we have a consistent way of contacting patients who are ninety days past due on bills, and is it working?

» Should we transition from paper to having patients fill out their dental history on tablets?

You can probably see that there are about 10,000 questions you could ask. But they're important questions that you won't ask when you're rushing through the day as both dentist and boss. By engaging in a deliberate documentation and prototyping process, you'll find all kinds of holes and weak spots in your business and you'll fix them.

This will also create a lot of work for you, and you'll have to repeat it when things change. For example, at Kids Dental Kare, we had an exhaustive process for handling paper records, and then we went paperless, with everything hosted at our enterprise data center and accessed via local servers. That meant we had a massive conversion process, but it was worth it.

All the while, you're writing your playbook, documenting every step, every decision, every success, and every failure. You can write things down on paper, enter findings into a database or app like Evernote, or do whatever you like, but keep in mind that when you grow bigger, your approved playbook will need to be part of your practice management software, so that anyone, anywhere can review it—including potential buyers or partners.

I used Linda Miles's training to develop my SOPs back when I first started, along with training from the Michael Gerber Institute. Linda taught me how to document SOPs and Gerber taught me how to think and document like an executive.

There's also a ten-step procedure documentation process[25] recommended by business process expert Denise O'Berry that I really like:

1. **Process Name**—Name the process. For example, try something like "associate performance reviews."

---

25 Denise O'Berry, "How to Document Your Current Processes in 10 Easy Steps," *Business 2 Community*, November 11, 2015, www.business2community.com/business-innovation/document-current-processes-10-easy-steps-01146390.

2. **Process Boundaries**—What triggers the process to start? How do you know when it's done?
3. **Process Outputs**—What does the process produce? In our example, it produces "a written, signed performance review with positives, areas for improvement, goals, and suggested actions, where appropriate."
4. **Process Inputs**—What's needed to implement this process and where does it come from?
5. **Process Activities**—What needs to be done to get the process from start to finish? This is free-form brainstorming time. For performance reviews, your list might include "set an appointment," "reserve a private meeting space," "create a documented, legally vetted performance review policy," "obtain a signed employment agreement indicating that the associate understands the policy," and "draft a performance review findings and recommendations form."
6. **Process Organization**—Sequence the activities from Step 5 into a process flow.
7. **Process Review**—Do a quality check. Based on the start and end points from Step 2, does the sequence of actions make sense? If not, make corrections.
8. **Process Roles**—Who's responsible for what in this process? Your HR person might be responsible for finalizing and vetting your performance review policy, but you as the dentist-owner will do the in-person reviews.
9. **Transcribe the Process**—Document everything, preferably using software.
10. **Final Process Review**—Review the process with everyone, get feedback, and get everyone's buy-in.

There's one piece that's missing, though: *testing*. I'm a big believer in testing your processes and procedures so you can find the points of failure early on. Do dry runs of everything, from billing to intake to training, and see where things fall apart. Where is communication not clear? Where do people not know what they're supposed to be doing? Where are associates standing around, not sure what treatment room to go to next?

If you can, you might even involve your patients in some testing to get invaluable feedback into what works and what flops. Be up front and tell them, "We're going to be trying a new digital records system that should let your dentist access your X-rays and dental records in seconds while you're in the chair—and also let her book your next appointment before you even leave the room. After your visit, we'd love your feedback on what worked and what didn't." People love to be asked for their opinion, and if you frame it as a process you're using to try to make their experience faster and better, your patients should be happy to help out.

A Proxy Version of You

This is where scripting different personal interactions for different locations can really help you decipher what works. In the Internet world, this is called A/B testing, and Google is famous for doing it with ads. Basically, once you have your processes documented, write different scripts for interactions at your two offices.

For example, when someone calls Office A, your receptionist says, "Thank you for calling Smith Dental, how can I help you?" When someone calls Office B, the receptionist says, "Thank you for calling Smith Dental, are you calling to confirm an appointment or schedule a new appointment?" Then see which greeting receives a more positive response from callers or helps your receptionist be more productive. You can A/B test everything: email, postcards, referral programs—you name it. Anytime you can create two versions of a process or procedure, do it and see which one comes out ahead. That's how you optimize efficiency and increase ROI.

But even processes that don't lend themselves to testing should be scripted, because you want predictability. You don't want your receptionists going off script, answering the phone and telling callers that you perform procedures that you don't, because now you've created expectations that you can't fulfill, and you look unprofessional when you have to backtrack and say, "Actually, we don't do orthodontics, but we can refer you."

All of this will help you immensely when you move from one office to two or two offices to three, because three offices is that threshold where the dentist-owner starts to become spread too thin. When you can no longer be everywhere at once, your documented procedures are a proxy version of you. They are there to enforce your way of doing things even when you're not on-site, so you can replicate what works at one office at another.

LUCRATIVE LARRY'S ADVICE ON . . . GOING PAPERLESS

Dr. Lanier went paperless with his practice's records and systems after already spending hundreds of hours putting it all down on paper, and it was a headache to make the switch. But today, paperless solutions are easy to find, easy to use, and cost-effective, so go paperless and cloud-based as soon as you can to save time and money. You'll give everyone involved in your practice easy, 24/7 access to important documents, be able to make changes fast, and have everything backed up in the cloud automatically.

Documentation Makes Training Easier

Having a documented plan for every activity and interaction that takes place within your offices makes training easier and faster. There's no ambiguity. The training manual (or playbook) gives associates and staffers the procedures in black and white. This can be important for associate dentists, because some will come in with a chip on their shoulder and the attitude that "I graduated from dental school—I don't have to follow your rules." Well, that's fine when you're in your house, but you're in mine. My house, my rules.

With Kids Dental Kare, I actually had my own training room, so I could bring all the managers and supervisors over and train them at my little headquarters. I started doing that after other training methods turned out to be frustrating. We would do webinars and hand them pads and paper, but nobody would even take notes. There was no way they were learning the material, and no way they would be able to drill it down to the people back at the office. I'd go to that office and see that people were still not following the procedures we'd just trained on. It was maddening. I'd have to keep repeating myself over and over, but that didn't always get better results.

Documenting and testing everything doesn't automatically make this compliance problem go away, but it can make it easier. One thing that does work is developing procedures *collaboratively*. Research shows that when people are involved in setting policies, they take more ownership of them and are more likely to implement them. If you get your staff's help in coming up with a system and working the bugs out of it, they're more apt to see it as theirs and to do what you ask them to do.

None of this is perfect, of course; operations is always frustrating for Entrepreneur Dentists because we're not trained in it. But you keep running plays and gaining short yardage, and you get better at convincing your people to do things your way. That's what I did.

DO

- **Be the dental equivalent of McDonald's fries.**
- **Put your head down and trust the plan.**
- **Insist on accountability and reporting.**

Be McDonald's French Fries

With documentation in place, and a model that can be replicated both at your current offices and at any new offices you open, you are ready to push the Start button on your plan. Keep in mind that the purpose of your plan at this point is to put as much of your business as possible on autopilot so that you can focus on building your brand and expanding.

The overall effect of putting your plan into motion should be a reassuring consistency at all your locations—even at mobile clinics. Your patients should be able to get the same experience at your location in Overland Park, Kansas, as they get at your office in downtown Kansas City, Missouri. That's why I like to say that you're creating the dental equivalent of McDonald's french fries. When you go to any McDonald's anywhere in the world, you can expect to get fries that taste the same, no matter what. That sort of predictability is comforting for patients and helps them—not to mention investors and lenders—to see you not only as another dentist but also as a polished, systematic business.

Consistency and standardization are also important for your team, especially when you get to five locations or more. Imagine your CFO or practice manager being able to go to any office in your franchise and find that the financials, personnel records, patient records, and everything else are done in exactly the same way as in every other office! Supplies are stored in the same place, and while marketing might be customized for the neighborhood, it's all coming from the same vendors and printers and being sent out by the same mailing service.

How much more efficient would your business be with that sort of predictability? How much money could you save by leveraging economies of scale if you were buying plastic cups and surgical masks for five practices from the same suppliers at the same time? How much less time would you or your practice managers waste correcting mistakes or retraining people because everything is documented and clear?

Take the next six months to set up predictable systems for legal, HR, billing and accounting, in-office procedures, marketing, social media, patient relationships and referrals, and the patient experience. Empower your practice manager to enforce the procedures and rules—and once you have a COO or other chief operations person, make him or her the ultimate authority on processes and procedures so you don't have to deal with it. Then put your head down and let consistency work its magic. After all, Shakespeare wrote, "Consistency, thou art a jewel."

Marketing

Since marketing is the most important ingredient in your success, you should be heavily involved in planning it. Hire a marketing agency to assist in your planning—and then to execute your plan. When you're small, it's better to choose one that's also small, because their overhead is lower and their fees won't be so high.

Choose a small advertising or marketing shop with experience developing strategies and tools for dental businesses, one that can provide services for branding, design, copywriting, social media management, and web and logo design—as well as manage your printing needs. Work with them to develop any marketing channels that you can't do yourself, like print and outdoor advertising, social media, collateral creation, website development, and writing radio ads.

But more important than paid advertisements is the organic presence you'll build through articles, images, videos, and related media that you and your staff can generate with the help of your agency. That's the kind of content you should be putting out every week, like clockwork.

Be sure to insist on regular reports so you can find out what's working. Anyone can spend your money and say, "Wait, give it more time." Get numbers and demand results. Also, when you're looking for a marketing agency, don't hire anyone on retainer. That's where you pay the agency a flat fee each month instead of paying them on a project basis. The cost predictability might seem nice, but people get complacent when they have a guaranteed stream of income. Better to keep your marketing people hungry and insist on getting their best work before you pay them.

At the same time, develop the tools you can manage with your own in-house marketing people: email newsletters, community outreach, speaking, etc. Then create a deployment calendar for mailers, email, ads, social media, public appearances, and all the rest—and then go.

Make your marketing run like a well-oiled machine, and don't worry about the results from day to day. Even the best marketing will probably take months to show substantial and consistent results. Repetition is the key, and it does work. Here's an example of that. At one point, I was doing everything, including television ads, billboards, and bus benches. My name was everywhere. I went to a place where I could order custom clinic jackets with my name on them, and the lady behind the counter asked me to write my name on the form. I wrote "Dr. Lanier."

She looked at me and said, "You're not Dr. Lanier. I see his advertising everywhere. Dr. Lanier's a white guy." I had to laugh. She had seen Dr. Lanier's name so much that I had her thinking I was white. I said, "Ma'am, I know who I am." Obviously, I was doing something right.

Technology

Technology is expensive, but what in dentistry isn't? Our job is to look at margins, and when I look at the margins of owning and using technology versus not using it, technology always comes out the winner. Stay current, but not too far ahead of the market, because you will wind up testing new products for everyone else.

The reason dental technology is generally worth the investment is because it makes life easier for you, your associate dentists, staff, and management. However, we have so many options for digital solutions that the landscape is bewildering. Because I didn't know a lot about technology early on, I tried to stick with products that I or my senior management staff were familiar with. But there's so much that's new, and so much that could be genuinely helpful, that it makes sense to plan on taking a few risks on new tech each year.

There are three facets to planning your technology investments. First, have a plan and a vendor for regular maintenance, so you can avoid downtime. Second, maximize uptime for the technology you currently use. Contract with a service provider that works with medical and dental practices. Here, the watchword is *routine*. You want your IT to work routinely, without any hiccups. If you notice your bandwidth speed at all, it's probably a bad thing.

Third, plan for regular upgrades. Not every new digital toy will be worth the cost, but it's still a good idea to find out about tools that might make you more productive and profitable. For example, digital diagnostics might give you a big edge over your competition if other dentists in your area aren't doing it yet, but a system that lets patients confirm appointments by text message might not yield enough cost savings to make it worth the software upgrades and training.

Get professional advice on technology, and get on a schedule for service and training on new applications. I recommend hiring either a full-time IT person or someone who will make you their sole client once you reach a volume that keeps them busy all the time. When your technology goes down, you have to stop work. Don't let that happen. Prevention is the best medicine.

Dental Techs

Speaking of dental technology, you have to have a smart dental tech on board. Find someone who has a sharp mechanical mind that you can train to work on your dental equipment—or even someone who already has experience, which is even harder to find. But once your pump or compressor goes down, you're in deep and have to shut down for the day. It could take days for your supplier to ship a replacement or send a repair person, and that will cost you a lot more than the fee for a good dental equipment tech.

Also, have a backup for everything, from compressors and vacuums to X-ray sensors and intra-oral cameras. They *will* fail on you from time to time, so have all your offices run on the same equipment when possible. That's smart standardization. Even if every office has a different look, they should have a lot of sameness when it comes to equipment and technology. That makes it easier to have someone on-site who knows how to switch out broken equipment. You cannot always wait on the tech from the equipment distributor to come out.

Have a storage facility, vehicles, and personnel to handle small issues. This is a prime example of where economies of scale come in. It doesn't make sense for a doctor with one or two offices to build a department like what I'm describing—or even a DSO with offices spread out over a wide area. But for those with offices close to each other, it makes perfect sense.

Referrals

What is your referral policy? Start with *asking for the referral* (AFR) as the end game. The word-of-mouth referral to family or friends is the most trusted referral you can get. That's how you test your customer service. If it's working, you'll get the referrals. But you have to have everyone scripted to do the right song and dance in order to move the patient into the "warm" referral category. Then you AFR before they leave the office. Have a tablet in hand and ask them on the spot for a referral, right after you've given them a carefully scripted, delightful, caring experience. More often than not, you'll get a "Yes, I'd be happy to."

Other things you can ask:

» "Did you enjoy your experience?"
» "Would you tell your family members or friends about us?"
» "Would you write us a review on Yelp or Google?"

What about text reminders to make referrals or give reviews? An online program to reward referrals with a code that gets the patient discounts for referring people? Referral requests on social media? Every one of those is worth trying.

However, keep in mind that constantly pumping people for referrals can become intrusive, and even insulting, if you overdo it. Show some restraint. Create a multi-component referral strategy—a monthly e-newsletter, a monthly mailer, and a post-appointment text message, for example—all linked to a patient rewards program. Then work that strategy. Have a goal of X referrals per month and track your results. Once you find a blend of elements that yields a steady flow of referral patients, lock it in.

Finances

Your financial plan starts with a CFO or CPA who can supervise it. Beyond that, plan on regular audits of your billing, accounts payable and receivable, insurance reimbursements, and the revenue produced by each of your associates. This is the time to check for irregularities and possible wasteful spending, too. Remember, "It's not how much you make, it's how much you keep."

What's your debt-to-equity ratio? How's your debt servicing looking? When do some of these large loans come due? How's the overall growth of the company vs. Office 1, Office 2, and beyond? What's your month-over-month same-store sales? What's the referral growth rate? New patient growth rate?

You or your financial advisors should be asking those questions on a quarterly basis. Finance's job is to advise on where you are, what to budget, and what to anticipate. This is management by statistics, and most of the statistics will come from your accounting software, dental management software, and specific metrics you've decided to measure on spreadsheets. Accounting is the main governor on the system, telling you when you're doing well or heading in the wrong direction.

Look at digital/paperless financial systems. Are you paying your employees by check when it would be easier and faster to pay them by direct deposit?

Will you offer patients payment options like Apple Pay? Now is the time to consider those.

Expansion

Since your growth will hinge on opening new locations, have a plan for learning about real estate and scouting for new locations. Most growth companies don't buy real estate because it ties up large amounts of cash (such as a thirty percent down payment). Fast growth requires liquidity, so almost all franchises lease their properties. But since they know that they will someday need to refinance or sell, they know that leases carry huge implications for the buyer. A poorly drafted, poorly negotiated lease that does not allow a new owner to step in and take over easily can be a nightmare.

Find a Realtor who has experience with medical and dental leasing—or even limits their practice to it. Get a great real estate attorney and go over your master plan. Develop a leasing plan with clear dos and don'ts.

Get on a regular schedule of traveling around to view possible properties. You should know where you want to go and why. Spend your time looking only at locations or sites in the specific area that fits your demographic and geographic profile. Have an "ideal property" profile written out, with all the specs that your ideal office would possess. Create a fact sheet for recording the relevant information about a property that looks like a good candidate: address, intersection, neighborhood, traffic patterns, parking, lighting, building size, number of offices, if it's already a dental office, who represents the owner, etc.

Remember, only a small percentage of the buildings you see will turn out to be realistic options, so finding your next location is about volume, volume, volume. Look at a lot of properties in a variety of places. Have a good commercial real estate broker on call,so when you find a potential location, you can move fast. Remember, the location is not for you; it's for your patients. Don't try to make it all about what's convenient to you—like down the street from where you live, just because you're too lazy to drive across town. If that is what you want, great. But is being expedient going to cost you a lot of money and compromise the vision?

Training and Accountability

Finally, have a set schedule for check-ins on every aspect of your business (especially finances) and for additional training. I'm talking about not only training on new procedures or systems but also refresher training. People get complacent about policies after a while, and things can start to slip. Regular training reminds them what the right way is and that you're holding them accountable for doing things your way.

Employees are notorious for saying, "I don't remember us training on that." Have training sign-in sheets documented and saved digitally so that if you're ever legally challenged, you can retrieve them to counter the claim that someone never received training.

Why invest in repeated training? Think of the axe-sharpening parable. Two men are in a tree-cutting contest and one stops in the middle to sharpen his axe, while the other keeps whacking away at the tree. The one who stops to sharpen his axe looks as though he's wasting time, but by the end of the contest, he's overtaken the guy who didn't—and goes on to win the contest. As you may remember, at the beginning of the book, I talked of my father being a logger with a side hustle sharpening the other loggers' saw blades. They all understood that when you make your living dropping trees all day, a sharp blade is everything.

Training is the same as sharpening those saw blades. It might seem to be a waste of productive clinical time, but when your staff members are sharpened and aligned with the same message and mindset—and properly handling procedures and compliance issues—you're prepared to win!

Also, have a standard schedule for employee performance reviews and include it in your employment contract. That way, everyone is accountable and nobody's surprised. Then it's your responsibility to actually do the performance reviews and not postpone them because you're too busy. I've heard about non-dental companies where employees have gone five years or more without a performance review. That can create a culture where nobody believes they're accountable or feels motivated to pursue excellence. As a small dental business, you can't afford to be that lax about feedback. Be as accountable to your people as you want them to be to you.

TALK TO THE EXPERT

My advice for those now engaged in building DSOs? Go forward with alacrity. Build your enterprise up to $25 to $50 million, and then be ready to partner or be acquired by a larger DSO. The opportunities for smaller DSOs at these $25 to 50 million revenue levels, in my view, are incredible. Getting to the $25 to 50 million level is a very hard climb, but will be well worth the struggle. Solo practices will become less and less attractive to the market, which will continue to push their asset value downward. Solo practices will not be able to keep pace with DSOs. They will lose their ability to recruit new dentists and staff. Solo practices will not be able to keep up with technology as it gets more and more expensive in terms of time and money. Their market share will continue to shrink.

So what should solo practices do? That is a whole other story, and not the focus of this article. But the further a dental practice moves toward DSOs on the business curve, and the further it occupies the late majority on the adoption curve, the fewer opportunities will exist for solo practices. The future is crystal clear: DSOs will dominate the industry.

According to my calculations, somewhere between 2025 and 2035, DSOs will be eighty percent of dental practices, not only in this country, but in all first-world countries. DSOs are certainly the future. There will be a half-dozen to a dozen very large players, but regional DSOs, partnered with these larger entities, appear to be in the lead. Know-how, capital, executive talent, and resources contributed by the larger entities to regional DSOs will powerfully support their growth and prosperity, without a significant loss of local authority.

—Marc Cooper, President/Partner of the DEO[26]

- **Build your reputation for great work.**
- **Adopt a service mentality.**
- **As Zig Ziglar advised, Get what you want by helping others get what they want.**

26 Dr. Marc Cooper, "A Look To The Future: How DSOs Are Changing the Landscape," Dentist Entrepreneur Organization, November 7, 2018, deodentalgroup.com/look-future-dsos-changing-landscape.

Your Reputation Is Everything

Executing your plan and having your processes running in the background, like the operating system of your dental business, frees you up to do what only you can: Build your reputation as a place that delivers great dental care and gives people a superlative experience. That's the foundation of your brand. If you support your marketing and branding by earning a wonderful reputation, you almost can't fail.

Always insist on the highest standards of quality care and service, without exception. Anyone who can't or won't conform to those standards has to go, because they can pollute your brand and harm your reputation. A reputation is like a giant redwood tree: It looks imposing, but it's surprisingly fragile, and a few well-placed blows can bring it crashing down.

Building a sterling reputation requires that you adopt what I call the *service mentality*. Yes, you're the boss. Yes, you spent years in dental school and are an expert. But in the end, it's your job to give patients an outstanding experience and to take pleasure in serving their needs. You're not just rendering dental service. You're making them feel comfortable and taken care of during what is (for some people) one of the scariest experiences they can have. They want to trust not only that you know what you're doing but also that you care about them and will pay attention to detail. That's what will get them to refer others to you.

That's a mental shift when you're used to being the boss. The patient becomes your boss. When you walk into the room, it's "I'm your servant, how can I help?" When you bring your kid to me, it's not about me being a doctor with years of experience; it's about me bending over backwards to take care of your precious child and give you both all of my attention. So yes, we're all servants . . . just well-paid ones!

"It takes 20 years to build a reputation and five minutes to ruin it. If you think about that you'll do things differently."

—WARREN BUFFETT

Make Yourself a Resource

Build your reputation by doing great work, treating people like you want to be treated, being honest and ethical, being the good guy, and becoming the dentist everybody recommends. Then repeat. Like marketing, building a reputation takes time; there are no shortcuts.

That's why it's so important to enjoy what you do as a dentist. If you love your work, it's contagious. If you hate your work, that's contagious, too. People will notice either way. If during the day, you're humming and singing, walking and smiling, it rubs off on other people. I really enjoyed dentistry, especially owning my own offices. I got a chance to play my own music—and I love music. I was always in charge of the sound systems in my offices. I always tried to keep the atmosphere fun and inviting for everybody. The kids felt it, and so did the parents.

You have to become conscious that every interaction with a patient has its consequences, either positive or negative. Everything affects your brand. The effects might not be obvious right away, but they will build up over time, like dental caries. The way your office looks, the front desk, the greeting, how you introduce yourself, the way you dismiss patients—everything will make an impression, like footprints in wet concrete. And like concrete, once those impressions set, they're hard to change. So get them right. Ask for the referral before the patient leaves. Say something positive about the patient. Make people feel good about seeing you.

The other thing you can do is make yourself a community resource. Do health fairs and in-school education sessions. Write articles about your field of dentistry. Answer patient questions, share insider information, give readers anything you think they might want to know. Go on local radio and do a Q&A. Answer questions on Facebook or Reddit. Stay in front of people to the point where they're sick of you; because when they have a question about anything involving dentistry, you want them to think, "I know, I'll go to Dr. Jones's blog."

All this is to serve your own interests, of course. Zig Ziglar said, "You can get everything in life you want if you will just help enough other people get what they want,"[27] and that's true. Dentists who want a clinical job? You help them get what they want. Assistants who want a job? You help them get what they want. Patients who need excellent dental care? You help them get what they want. Just keep helping other people get what they want and, over time, you'll get more and more of what you want, too.

By the way, in case you're tempted to dismiss this reputation stuff . . . there's an industry rule of thumb that says that eighty to eighty-five percent of the saleable value of a dental practice comes from the goodwill that its patients hold for it. Reputation matters . . . a lot.

---

27 Zig Ziglar, *Zig Ziglar's Secrets of Closing the Sale* (Old Tappan, NJ: F. H. Revell Co., 1984).

EYEING THE EXIT

The more systematic and documented your business is, the more attractive it is likely to be to a buyer. Investors want profit machines, so unless you sell to another dentist, your buyer won't have the knowledge to ensure that patients are receiving the best care. You'll need to ensure that with procedures and policies you already have in place.

Keep in mind that your brand has saleable value, too. Your brand is the sum total of your reputation, and if it's well known and has desirable qualities associated with it—dependable, expert, honest, great service, great with kids—that tells buyers that you will probably keep most of your patients even after you exit the practice. That's reassuring, because no buyer wants a forty percent falloff in business after a sale. So build your brand by keeping your marketing machine running and doing things the right way.

CHAPTER 8

Grow What You've Made

CHECK YOUR GPS

You're ready to grow and establish a plan that will take your business into the clouds. Let's make sure you're on the right runway:

- **Deliberately define your destination**: What elements of your plan will you lock down first? (Financial, HR, and patient interactions might be good places to start.)
- **Lock it into your internal GPS**: What resources do you need to put your plan into action? What actions will you take to build your reputation and make yourself a dentistry resource?
- **Choose an ETA**: When do you want to hit Start on certain automated elements of your plan, such as marketing and referrals, and how long will you let them run until you check the results?
- **Devise your plan**: What are your revenue goals for the first year after you get your plan in motion?
- **Get started now**: Begin locking down processes and procedures for every dimension of your business.
- **Trust the plan and keep moving.**

By the time I got to fourteen Kids Dental Kare locations and almost $20 million in revenue, I had a number in mind. I wrote down that number in Fiji. I had paid about $10,000 to travel to Tony Robbins's resort down there. Actually, it's more of a high-end training facility for entrepreneurs, and I thought it would give me the secret sauce I needed to get me to my exit.

While I was there, Tony had a session where you had to sit down and write out your *number*: both how much you wanted to exit with and when. It wasn't until after I finally exited that I realized it: *The number I'd walked away with was the number I'd written down!* It was like putting that number in my mind made it happen.

Not enough Entrepreneur Dentists work on that number. I've seen some blow the notion off when you mention it to them. But having that goal in mind really does make a difference, because when you orient your mind on how much you need to grow, you're more likely to make it happen. I talked to Tony quite a few times and I said, "You'd better be right, because I'm drinking your Kool-Aid!"

He'd say, "Keep drinking it." If you do, and you try to implement the things that you're taught, and you're setting goals, you will get closer and closer, until you realize that you've gotten where you wanted to be. You can even adjust and course-correct and still get there. But it will only happen if you grow.

You might want to focus on your exit. But in doing dentistry, it's easy to be lulled into complacency, like someone on a beach just standing and watching a wave roll in, until he realizes that what he thought was a small wave is actually a monster that knocks him down and drags him under. By the time you know what's happening, it's too late.

Because most dentists fail to develop an exit strategy, they are confined to working in the practice until they retire. Most will retire when the practice is on the downslope, with diminished revenues, older equipment, an older office design, etc. If you sell at that point, you will get much less money than if you had planned for a proactive, strategic exit.

You want to exit when you're at your peak, not spend the rest of your days regretting that you failed to prepare and optimize for the sale and pull the trigger when you had the chance. The problem is a consistent one: Too many dentist-owners don't have a growth strategy. They don't understand that exiting means growing, because buyers look for a business that's profitable but also shows a strong, consistent growth trend. Healthy businesses grow; unhealthy ones contract. If you want to exit rich, your growth strategy and your exit strategy must be one and the same.

THINK

- **There are two ways to add locations.**
- **Replicate past successes.**
- **Have a rainy-day fund saved.**

Buy or Build?

Before you do anything else, know your number. Seriously. How much do you want to walk away with after you sell? $10 million? $20 million? Talk to your personal financial advisor to learn about what you can net after the sale of your business—and what you'll need to live on for the rest of your life.

Once you have that number in mind, sit down with an investment banker or your CFO and find out what businesses the size of the one you're running right now are selling for. That gives you your starting point. Next, it might be worthwhile to get a professional valuation of your business. This is expensive—typically, anywhere from $5,000 and up, depending on the complexity of your operation—but it can help you determine how much you need to grow to reach your goal. Try contacting a CFO with mergers-and-acquisitions experience in the dental world to get an appraisal.

Once you know all this—your number, your current valuation, and how much you need to grow to reach your number—there's only one relevant question you should be asking:

"How many locations do I need to add?"

Dental businesses grow by serving more patients, and they do that by adding offices. If you use the rough estimate that each office, run optimally, will generate about $2 million in revenue per year, you can do the math. But whether you need to go from two locations to ten or from ten to twenty, you only have two options: Build new locations from scratch, *de novo*, or acquire an existing practice.

I never acquired another dentist's practice. I did buy two offices that were built out, but we didn't get any patient lists or anything else. But even that didn't work out well. Those offices underperformed. The problem I have with buying someone else's practice is that you can become so enamored with the idea that it's turnkey that you ignore the fundamentals that have made you successful, like location. Does the practice you're trying to acquire align with your current practice mix? How long will the owner stay on to run the practice? Will you have to change out their entire software system?

According to your plan, you want a certain part of town, a certain level of density, a certain level of visibility. If those criteria have worked for you at all of your other locations, but you violate them now just because someone else has an office that's ready to go, you're going against a proven model. Also, what will it cost to bring the building up to your standards? You don't want to overspend; avoid doing $500,000 in renovations to a house on a block where the other houses cost $300,000.

For *de novo* expansion, try to build new locations from scratch, using your first ones as a prototype. That lets you put location first and choose the density, visibility, convenience, and presentation that suit your brand and fit your niche. That's brand consistency.

Acquisition growth is a very viable model used by many of the larger DSOs. The problem is that many entrepreneurs and investors use the "duct tape" approach. They get several groups of dissimilar practices and jam them together in a group—even though they may not have any synergies or alignment, except that they're dental offices. That might be good for leveraging economies of scale, but it's not a philosophy for building a platform.

If You're Going to Expand, Do It Right

Building from scratch makes sense because you already know how to do it. You already have the formula for building a profitable office: your business model, your plan, and your pattern of hiring good people. Follow the plan and let the business model guide you.

That said, if you're going to open a new location, do it right. When you've been on a winning streak, it can be tempting to coast. Maybe you could let the parking lot at this next office slide a bit. Maybe the waiting area chairs could be IKEA instead of the usual expensive ones you have in your other offices. Right?

Wrong. Remember, everything you do either reinforces or contradicts your brand, especially your facility. Be ready to invest enough money to have that new facility looking like it's part of a national brand. You want patients to walk in and find something spotless, professional, and beautiful. You want to make an impression.

Don't get too clever. Simply replicate everything you've done at your other locations. I do recommend doing a viability study on the location before you commit, though. Find out if the area and demographics can provide the revenue you need. Can you find doctors in the area? What will your costs for build-out and operations be? Does the property have the square footage to accommodate the number of offices and patient traffic you need? If the figures look good, pull the trigger on the deal.

I'll put it in doctor's language. Rx: Growth. Sig: Rinse and repeat as directed, according to your deliberate plan. It really can be this simple, especially when you have a strong team: lawyer, lender, real estate broker, and contractor. When you have a business model that works, use it as your filter. Run every aspect of a possible new office through that filter, and if any aspect of the location isn't a fit, walk away. Better to wait to open an office than expand into a spot that's going to become a financial drain. When a location does fit, trust your model and your people and make it happen once, twice, five times, and more. That's how you build something big.

One more thing: When you're doing something like adding a location, have a little rainy-day fund set aside for when things go wrong. Because they will. I made plenty of mistakes in my career and cost myself plenty of money, but I managed to stay alive after all of them because I always followed my mother's advice: "Save something for a rainy day." Even in Los Angeles, rainy days happen.

DO

- **Constantly be recruiting, training, mentoring, and monitoring (RTMM).**
- **Be careful with financing.**
- **Stick with one new office at a time for now.**

Recruiting, Training, Mentoring, and Monitoring

This is where even an otherwise-dauntless Entrepreneur Dentist can get nervous. When you start growing aggressively, you undertake a big responsibility. You have to make sure everybody on the ship arrives safely. You're taking on more liability, and the stakes are higher—but you've got this. You already know how to do this. Even though you're taking on more risk, it's calculated risk.

I would rather bet on myself than go to Vegas. After all, I built the model. It's predictable. Certain inputs that I know very well—number of patients, number of associates, and marketing expenditures—will lead to predictable outputs, just as surely as sunshine, water, and dirt lead to grass. You're the same. You built your prototype. You know what works. Scale changes nothing except your anxiety level.

What makes the entire process easier is an emphasis on what I call RTMM:

» Recruiting
» Training
» Mentoring
» Monitoring

Those four activities never stop. Each time you launch a new location, you're recruiting associates, assistants, and staff. You're training them in the procedures and processes that you've been documenting and fine-tuning for years. You're coaching and advising them in becoming a profitable team. And you're monitoring their performance and the financial health of the new office. Then you move to the next new location and you go through that whole process again.

Those four activities make opening profitable offices not only possible but also predictable. I became such a devotee of efficient training during my expansion that I even created online training modules for my people. Everything involved in running a Kids Dental Kare office was online. There were instructional videos, test questions, and systems that would tell me how much of a video someone had watched. Every time we hired someone new, they would go through the online training and we could test them after it was finished. We could repeat it until they got the process right.

If you can make recruiting, mentoring, and monitoring that systematic and automatic, you can save yourself from being stretched too thin and still get great results in new offices. For example, for recruiting, use tools like Indeed and ZipRecruiter, which send you pre-screened job candidates. Mentoring doesn't have to come from you; by the time you've grown a substantial business, your practice manager, and perhaps some associate dentists, probably have the experience and wisdom to mentor new hires. Monitoring can be a simple matter of an online financial dashboard. In other words, you can do this.

Building a Business That's System-Dependent

At this stage, you're thinking about the big picture, and that's good. You have your operations person, practice managers, and others to deal with the granular things. You should have your eyes on growth and a prosperous exit. However, you can't bury your head in the sand. You are still the one who decides what's important. It's your business.

Once, early on, I let some guys sell me some signage for the front of my building. It looked like a good deal until I placed the order, and then I found out that I was overpaying. I tried to cancel and they said, "No, we already started production on it." When they said the sign was ready, I said, "I'm not going to pay for it." They took me to court, but I ignored the entire matter.

Bad idea. Next thing I knew, my bank account was being garnished for the cost of the sign. So I said, "Well, send me the sign." They had destroyed it, they said, but because they had stored it for six months, I owed them the cost of storage. The whole thing was a fiasco, and it was my fault. I didn't take responsibility for what was in front of me.

You're the business owner. Everything starts and stops with you. People want to know that you've seen the file, signed off, given your opinion, made the call. You determine what's important and what isn't worth your time—but someone has to be at the wheel. Every organization has to have a leader, but it doesn't have to be you.

A core principle of growth is to make the founder expendable. You build your model so that you, personally, can walk away; it's your position that's *not* expendable. That's what I did: I built an organization that, while it may have relied on me, would be completely able to function and turn a profit if I was run over by a bus next Thursday. That's why when we created an organizational board for the company, we didn't put down names, only positions.

My org board started with money management and marketing. Below money, we had the finance department, controller, bookkeeping, and the bookkeeping assistant. I had an operations manager, regional managers, general assistants, and so forth. But no names. The message is simple: *Everybody is replaceable*. The system is what's important, because if someone leaves, it's what ensures that patients get taken care of, money comes in, and each position is filled by competent, trained staff.

When you can go from being people-dependent to system-dependent, you become valuable to a buyer. When you reach a point where you have such well-honed systems and training in place that you can lose almost anyone, plug anyone into the same job, and have them making you profitable in a matter of days, you're in the exit zone. That is a well-oiled machine.

By the way, none of this is to say that people don't matter. They matter very much. Remember, goodwill is the most important piece of a dental business's valuation, and that comes from caring, committed people. The point here is that losing someone won't bring down your business. With a strong model running, the business will survive and recover. People leave, retire, move, and die. No buyer wants a business dependent on people staying forever. Buyers want companies that can outlive their founders.

LUCRATIVE LARRY'S ADVICE ON . . . FINANCING

Money is still cheap, even though rates have gone up in the last year. That means if you can get a loan, save your cash and finance your new location. Like Dr. Lanier said, banks love to lend to dentists because the default rate is so low, but after a few locations, when goals and loan amounts get bigger, many banks get skittish. However, there are some banks willing to work with expanding practices, and other bodies exist to lend to dental businesses. Organizations like the ADSO or DEO can be good sources of information about reputable lenders.

Financing Expansion

Get that FICO score up to at least 720 as soon as you can. Watch your credit score like your life depends on it, because it does, especially in the beginning, when everything is dependent upon your ability to borrow. Banks are not very good at assessing how creative and smart you are, so they depend on things they can measure.

How do you finance all this expansion, build-out, and hiring? Well, if you're starting out and your credit score is poor, you can work for someone else and save the money you need to open your own office. Otherwise, you'll wind up paying very high rates or borrowing from some unscrupulous company with all kinds of prepayment penalties and loan shark–like interest rates.

That being said, now is one of the best times in history to borrow. Banks love dentists and are quite willing to loan to first-time dentists. Most dentists can repay this loan if they stick to one office. Banks know that dentists get very little financial training, so they get a little worried when we start asking to expand. They want to know what you did with the last loan they gave you.

This reminds me of the parable in Matthew 25, when the messiah tells of a man who gave talents (money) to his servants before leaving on his journey: "To one he gave five talents, to another two, to another one, according to his ability." Two of the servants doubled their master's money, but the servant who got just one talent buried it. The first two received a "Well done, my good and faithful servant," while the one that didn't do anything with his allotted talent was called a "wicked and slothful servant."[28]

The point is, the banks will want to see how you performed, and your financials will be your report card. If you haven't done anything to grow the last loan you received, they will be unlikely to loan you more. They will also want to know if you're growing too fast.

Another option is to self-finance. With one office of your own, you can generate so much profit that you can finance the next one yourself. The average well-run dental office might operate at a twenty percent margin. If you could maintain that, and your office brought in $600,000 in gross revenue for the year, $120,000 of that would be profit. That's outrageous. With that kind of profitability, you could self-fund your expansion.

---

28 Matthew 25:26, KJV.

But if money is cheap, as it still is now, don't burn your cash. Save that for a rainy day. Grab financing and just keep expanding. If you don't have any problems with your FICO score, borrowing could be your best option. For a larger dental business, lenders tend to finance 100 percent of equipment costs and maybe 50 percent of your build-out costs. If you've got some cash reserves from your existing office to use for build-out and initial marketing, you're in business.

But there's another option that you should avoid—and it just so happens that I know that because I tried it. When I started Kids Dental Kare, I had been out of work because I relocated and took a little while to pass the California board exam. By the time I opened the doors, my FICO score was down below my knees; I couldn't get an apple on credit. So I started taking "hard-money" loans with interest rates up to twenty-two percent.

Trust me: You don't want that money. You think, "I'll get on my feet and I'll pay it off." But it's not that easy. You could pay the balance off after a year, but you're paying interest for the whole term of the loan. Avoid hard-money loans completely if you can. Instead, increase your chances of getting a legitimate loan by doing two things. First, bring in your CFO. A business finance pro will keep your books clean and pretty so that lenders can look at them and say, "This person is following good business principles. He's a good risk." Pay for good financial guidance up front.

Second, present a solid business plan. A plan that shows your growth rate and schedule for expansion (*pro forma*) is a vital document. It should include the following:

» **Executive summary**—This is a one-page summary of your business, including revenue goals, operating processes, marketing strategies, and financial data.

- **Description of your business**—Explain what type of practice you are building: general dentistry, pediatric, cosmetic, etc.
- **Marketing**—How you will let people who live in your service area know about your practice? Detail the methods and strategies you'll use, from social media to referral programs to public appearances.
- **Management team and system**—Provide detailed bios of the key leaders and management personnel who make your office go. That could include your practice manager, associates, assistants, hygienists, and more. Also detail your management system and its processes and procedures.
- **Financials**—Plan on providing a break-even analysis, cash flow projections, sample balance sheets, and profit-and-loss statements.
- **SWOT analysis**—Lenders will want to see a realistic comparison between you and your competitors, categorized into Strengths, Weaknesses, Opportunities, and Threats (SWOT). Be clear about how you will differentiate yourself from competitors in your new market.

With the proven profitability of dental enterprises, if you can show that you're prepared to invest some of your own money in the expansion, and you've painted a picture of a solid, well-run business that's already profitable, you should be able to find solid funding.

So You Want to Buy an Existing Practice . . . ?

But let's say that you don't want to build a location from the ground up. You want to expand faster to leverage a gap in the market or take advantage of cheap money, and you want to purchase an existing dental practice. What should you look for?

First, be prepared to spend more than you would to build a new office because, of course, you're going to want to acquire a well-run practice, and that will cost you. Still, it's worth the premium price, because you don't want to come in and fix offices that are poorly run and have entrenched staff who won't cooperate with you.

You're looking for a practice that's well run and has good patient flow, and then you want to bring in your best practices and standardize things. But you also have to insist on something that suits your model for location, appeal, and efficiency. You will almost certainly have to bring in some new people, since some of the staff (and even associates) at the acquired practice won't be interested in following your processes and procedures. That's another way in which acquisition is more trouble than it's worth.

However, acquiring offices with different specialties can help you diversify your portfolio. You can offer general dentistry in one location, cosmetic in another, and orthodontics in a third, all while having centralized billing, marketing, and even phones. Meanwhile, your original locations can keep focusing on their specialization and niche.

But acquisitions are tricky—ask any CEO who's merged public companies and tried to blend cultures and management philosophies. You have a model, and now there's another successful dentist who's got his own way of doing things. The DSO model might be the best option for acquisitions: Handle administration and the back office, monitor finances, and then let the doc run things the way he did before you came along. Bring in best practices where you can and adapt.

How Many Locations?

I hear this question frequently from Entrepreneur Dentists who have launched multiple locations and think they have growth all figured out: "Should I open multiple locations at once?" My answer is always the same: "No, not until you have a perfect system and a solid source of funding."

Most of the time that I was running Kids Dental Kare, I started one location at a time. I did open several within a short period, however, and near the end, I opened three new offices at once. You become more experienced as you develop your organization and your own skills as a manager and entrepreneur. If you open three offices and one office flops, the other two might generate enough cash flow to keep you from defaulting on your loan. There will occasionally be one that will not work, regardless of your plans. But when you have enough revenue streams spread out across your platform, you'll be okay.

If you want to open more than one new office, you'll only become a solid risk for a lender when you can show a portfolio of six, seven, or maybe eight offices, all running like Swiss watches and raking in revenue. If you have your system and your team in place, it's possible. But you should also have a relationship with a banker you trust. If you've borrowed from the same bank while you've been opening one office at a time, there's a good chance that they'll lend to you for multiple offices. But remember what I said earlier: After about $5 million, some banks get skittish. If that happens, some bigger institutions like Wells Fargo or Bank of America have a dental loans department, and if they know you and your business, there's a good chance they'll want a piece.

There's another funding option here, too, but it's trickier to navigate: *private equity*. As you grow and prove that you can generate profits, people will want to partner with you, especially other dentists. I tried this for a short time. A couple of my employees bought stock, but it didn't work out, and I wound up paying them a lot of money to get my stock back.

The tricky thing about partnerships is that everyone who puts in money wants to have a say in how things are run, and that doesn't work. You might want somebody's money, but you don't want them running the show. You need a contract that says you're the controlling partner. You're the one with the system and the experience, and anyone who won't agree to that doesn't buy into the company. The problem I encountered is one that should have been apparent early on; I definitely would have caught it if I hadn't been under the pressure of the situation I had put myself into by growing too fast. That problem was dilution. They weren't willing to put in more time or money, and I had to put in more of both, while they benefited. A well-designed and well-negotiated agreement by someone with experience in mergers and acquisitions would have saved me from that problem.

Private equity can be scary, because you can lose control of what you've spent years building. There are plenty of horror stories of small business owners being maneuvered right out of their boxer shorts and losing controlling interest in their companies. That's why you don't make a move without careful vetting by your attorney and CFO. Then, if you're ready, selling equity in your business can really make sense.

I was talking to a doctor who wanted to know about exit strategies, but he was saying, "I'm not ready to get out of here. I'm not ready to retire." He liked working and the people he worked with. So I said, "You don't have to retire, but you can sell off part of your equity and cash out some of your hard work; you'll still have a relationship with your people and you can still be a dentist. Later on, you can sell the rest and get a second bite of the apple." That's what he did.

Whether you're looking at banks, other lenders, or private equity, opening multiple offices at the same time is a big, complex undertaking. It's something you should probably wait to do until you're near the end—until you're three offices away from your big cash-out goal. But do educate yourself on the process. Then, go for it.

KEEP IN MIND

- **There are jackals out there who will attack you.**
- **The business model matters more than any person.**
- **Keep your eye on the bottom line.**

The Model Is Everything

The downside of all this success and money is that with it comes a collection of jackals who will try to pick the flesh off your bones. You're leveraging other people's time and money, and you have to watch very closely, especially when other doctors are billing under your brand. You have to protect yourself. If you see that things are going wrong, pull the trigger, because anything an unscrupulous doctor does could wreck your model.

One of the things that most people don't think about is that when you start growing and expanding fast, you suddenly have a lot of debt servicing. If something goes wrong, suddenly you can't keep up. People will start picking you off. Word gets around. If you're having problems, even temporarily, the jackals will surround you.

When things are shaky and your attention is divided between dentistry and putting out fires, other dentists can solicit your patients—or even steal away your management team. Fire them immediately. Good doctors are hard to find, but bad ones are easy to replace. Pull the trigger because anything they do could wreck your business model, and while every individual is expendable, the model is everything. The business model is your future.

Eyes on the Prize

The model is so important at this stage because you're close to your exit—maybe only a year or two away. So at this point, making a clean, wealthy exit should be your only focus. Here's how to start planning for it:

» ***Take advantage of economies of scale.*** If you haven't up to now, add to your margins a little by purchasing the supplies and services you need as one business, not a collection of separate offices, and then distribute what you get to the various offices. That will reduce costs, which is one of the things you're after at this stage.

» ***Document all your systems, policies, and procedures.*** A buyer should be able to come in and, with a little study, get things running again.

» ***Know your number.*** If you have a wealth manager or certified financial planner, this might be the time to invite them to lunch to talk about what you'll need to sell your business for in order to afford the lifestyle you want. I had no plans of downsizing my lifestyle after retiring, so I needed as much as—or more than—I was already spending. I deserve it and so do you.

» ***Rivet your attention on costs and the bottom line.*** Take a hard look at your margins. I aimed for a twenty-five percent margin the entire time I was running Kids Dental Kare, and that was possible because I was operating an efficient, well-run business. Running that sort of margin gives you room to increase compensation for your dentists, for example, and still keep a solid twenty percent margin.

But maintaining a healthy margin means having a laser eye on costs, especially unnecessary ones.

Once, a friend asked me to check out his office in New Orleans. He had gone out and bought all Siemens equipment, the most expensive dental equipment you could buy. It was running $25,000 or $30,000 per operatory, while mine was running around about $7,000 per operatory for first-line equipment. Has a patient ever asked you what brand of equipment you use? No. Because they don't know or care. But when you waste money on things like that, you're debt-servicing. That doesn't look good. Now is the time to pay attention to what investors are looking for.

Your goal is to build a turnkey profit machine, which will give you a saleable asset and more freedom to enjoy wealth. Now, let's look at the final stage in this journey: the exit.

EYEING THE EXIT

This is the time to make sure that you have a strong, independent management team in place to attract the right buyer. Buyers want to know that they can acquire your company without it missing a beat, and an effective management team is a huge part of continuity.

Your practice manager will be a vital part of this deal, but you may also want to consider bringing on a full-time CFO and an operations person, to make sure financials are perfect and the business is running smoothly. If you're at ten offices and a potential $15 million payday, you can afford to pay out some salary and give up a little equity for some steady, veteran hands who can give you the expertise and support you need.

CHAPTER 9

Plan for Your Exit

CHECK YOUR GPS

You're ready to grow but may be unsure what kind of growth makes the most sense. It's time for one last course correction.

- **Deliberately define your destination**: What's your number? What do you need to be able to sell your business for in order to walk away with enough cash to fund your lifestyle?
- **Lock it into your internal GPS**: How many offices will you need to open to build a business with that kind of valuation?
- **Choose an ETA**: What is your target date for selling? What's your schedule for opening New Office 1, New Office 2, and so on?
- **Devise your plan**: Will you build new locations from scratch, or is there a compelling reason to acquire existing offices? Have you secured a funding source?
- **Get started now**: Start pulling together the documentation you'll need to get funding, including clean financials and a clear business plan.
- **Trust the plan and keep moving.**

Finally, you've made it! You've built a dental business with multiple locations, a staff of trained professionals, and a cash flow in the tens of millions. You're ready to . . . well, if not lie on a white sandy beach somewhere, certainly ready to sell what you've built for a lot of dough and start the next act of your life, a well-earned new chapter after years and years of work.

You're ready to exit. So let's talk about how to do that. There are lots of companies that we would have never expected to go belly up that wound up in bankruptcy last year, and several big ones this year. Remember, the money isn't yours until it's in your bank account.

First of all, this is something you plan on years in advance, but I expect you already know that. That's why we've talked about documentation and growth and knowing your "number." Exiting rich is a deliberate process of putting things in order and moving closer and closer to the final step. You have to know that this is the time. Right now, dentistry is one of the hot topics in the area of mergers and acquisitions, so it's a good time to go to market for those who are properly prepared.

That's why you've been prototyping and working on the business model. That's why you've been growing: because you have to scale to a certain amount before you'll catch the interest of the real players. There are some buyers who will look at a company doing only $10 million in top-line revenue, but they are few and far between. There are a few more who'll look at companies doing $20 million, $30 million, and $100 million, and others that will not touch anything less than that. You have to know who's looking where you're living.

Since the end of the dot-com era in 2001, everybody and their mother has approached me about doing some type of "roll up," involving me putting my company inside theirs and taking it to market, where I would get stock from their company. I never took the bait, but a couple years later, I would always hear about that company going bankrupt or the founder going to prison for some scam. I'm a backwoods country boy, but it ain't my first day at the rodeo. Don't hand your hard-earned equity to some scammer. Have an exit plan and don't waste time or energy meeting with characters who would even suggest such an idea.

You also need to be prepared to deal with investment bankers. They are specialists in valuing and selling businesses. If you want real money, you pay for an investment banker, because they know how to take you to market. After you get past two or three practices, investment bankers will be your only option when it comes time to sell.

That time came for me in 2017. Kids Dental Kare was ready for market. I had considered selling to private equity, because my asking price was not something that most other Entrepreneur Dentists would be prepared to pay. I had even tried approaching private equity companies myself, but found that's not a task for a business owner to handle alone. Luckily, I had read the book *Why Should White Guys Have all the Fun?* by Reginald Lewis. It was a motivational read for me because Lewis was the first black billionaire in America; and in the book, he talked about the mergers and acquisitions he and Michael Milken went through. I was encouraged and felt like I was ready to tackle my exit.

The Team

By the time I got close to my exit, I had a wealth management advisor, and when I mentioned it to him, he said, "Oh yeah, no problem, Doc. We can line some companies up and set up interviews, and you can decide who you want to go with." Just like that. He helped me source some investment bankers, and I wound up with a small group that had done quite a few health-care deals, but hadn't done dental yet. I tell you, it's funny how the resources just magically appear when you have a lot of money. I guess that's why money just keeps on making money, or it should, at least.

The investment bankers wanted a retainer, but the percentage was much lower than a dental broker—a real estate salesperson who sells dental practices—would have asked for, and they got a higher percentage if they exceeded my minimum price. We negotiated that. It worked out to $15,000 down and $10,000 a month, plus their commission once we sold. There's nothing wrong with people being incentivized to make more money for themselves, because they're going to make more money for you, too. No, I didn't want to pay that kind of money without any guarantee of a sale at the end, but I had to weigh the risks against the rewards. The ROI looked good and it was something I knew I could not do myself. So I hired a great team to get the price I wanted.

You'll want to have your walk-away price in mind. That's the price below which you will not sell. Since you're selling when your practice is at the top of its game, if you can't get your price, you have to be prepared to keep on operating and settling for that measly multimillion-dollar income. There are worse fates. You can always keep growing and try again in a couple of years, when the conditions are better.

When I started talking to investment bankers, and they looked at my number, they said, "You're going to have to bring in a CFO, and it's not going to be cheap. Are you willing to spend the money to put the numbers together and find out where you are?" I was. I didn't know exactly where I was, but I had a good feeling. I'd always operated from a profit mentality and tried to control costs and keep margins strong. I always had a line in the sand where I said to myself, "If I give away this or I accept that, I might as well go back to working for somebody else." You have to know where that line in the sand is as far as spending, paying people, or being charitable.

Often, especially in dentistry and medicine, people seem to think we should be altruistic, and I try to be, but money is the reason we're in business. The only way to keep score is by checking the financials—not only counting the money passing through but also seeing what you've kept. The numbers are how you navigate and stay on course, both across your entire business and from one office to another. So I had a good idea of what I was keeping, and I knew I was growing and profitable, and I had clean financials and strong, documented procedures so the business could run without me. But I still didn't know exactly where I was. That's why I needed the CFO.

I brought somebody in, and he and his team converted my accounting from cash to accrual and then went through my financials with a fine-tooth comb. It was definitely *not* cheap, but I was pleasantly surprised. The CFO was actually kind of shocked. He said, "Your numbers are pretty good. I didn't expect that." With most dentists, he would have been right. That's why that profit mentality is so important. It won't steer you wrong.

Getting to Close

Now I was able to start looking at my "multiple," meaning the multiple of EBITDA that I might be able to sell for. EBITDA is the standard metric of business valuation, and it means earnings before interest, tax, depreciation, and amortization. A valuation of your company will tell you what your EBITDA is, and then the health of the business and the industry you're in will give you an idea of what multiple of that number you can hope to sell for. For example, if your EBITDA is $3 million, and you, your investment banker, and your buyer agree that your multiple should be five, then your business will sell for $15 million.

The healthier your business, the higher your multiple will be. Some of the factors that can increase your multiple include—

» High margins

» Consistent single-store revenue growth

- Consistent year-over-year revenue growth
- Low debt
- Healthy patient and community goodwill
- A clear, well-documented system to operate the business
- A strong management team
- Clean financials
- Strong marketing and referral programs
- A well-maintained patient database
- Owning your locations
- Being in a growth industry

You can't control the last one, but you can control all the others. That's why it's so important to maintain a profit mindset and a marketing mentality. It all leads to this. When the CFO and investment bankers saw my operation, we determined that my multiple was seven, which was higher than I ever could have hoped for. We met with some potential buyers, and in the end, I ended up selling my fourteen locations to Western Dental in August 2017.

Because I didn't sell to private equity, I didn't even have to stay on as CEO for a year or two as part of the deal. I just had to be available to advise and consult on how to run things, and they didn't even ask me to come to the office! I was free. I was out. At sixty-two years young, I was ready for the next chapter.

THINK

- **Is it time to exit?**
- **Your family will probably not want to buy your business.**
- **Your job is to make yourself expendable.**

Is It Time?

You might be ready for your exit, or you might still be working and enjoying yourself. You might not be sure what you want. But when you are ready, I'm going to show you what to do.

First of all, how do you know when it's time to sell? Truth be told, sometimes you don't. Someone approaches you and asks you about selling, which is a compliment, because you know you've built something of value. That's common, because when you're working on the business and working on growth, you might not even be paying attention to what you're creating. I didn't join the ADSO for years, even though I had passed the minimum $10 million threshold years earlier, because, frankly, I didn't realize that I'd passed it. I knew what I was generating, but it didn't occur to me to stand back and say, "I have a $10 million business." You can keep your nose so close to the grindstone that you lose sight of everything else.

Exiting is a wake-up call. I'd say when the work stops being fulfilling, it's time to exit. The money you make along the way in dentistry is good. If you have a good product, you're going to have enough money to live well, but you'll be trading your time for money. When you can't make yourself do that anymore, it might be time to hang up your handpiece. When you have a new goal that looks nothing like building dental offices—such as starting a new business, building a house somewhere different, traveling, or starting a jazz combo with your kids and playing the acoustic bass (my dream)—it's probably time to leave.

Outside forces might also hustle you out the door. If the market for dental businesses is red-hot and prices are high, the chance to make big money might be too good to pass up. So you say, "I can always sell and start a new practice." You might have a non-compete clause to deal with, but there are ways around those—so yes, you can do that. And even if you're not ready to walk away entirely, you can sell some of your equity and keep working part-time, or be like my friend who works for a DSO and spends a lot of time playing golf. There are a lot of ways to keep your hand in dentistry without the long hours and stress of actually running the show. If that's your cup of tea, great.

If you decide that it's time to exit, just make sure that you exit with enough money that you never have to go back to work if you don't want to. You'll have enough money to sustain you and your family through your retirement and your next act. There's nothing sadder in my profession than seeing a dentist who was careless with his profits and didn't build a system—and then reached a point where he had to leave, sold for what he could get, and had to come back because it wasn't enough. I have a friend, also a dentist, and he and I used to talk a lot. I always asked him, "Do you have any associates helping you?" I was curious if anybody was helping him grow his business into something he could sell.

"No," he would say. "I only trust myself." I would always think, "Man, that's going to be hard." Unfortunately, I was right. When it came down to it, he couldn't even sell the practice. It had no value. He sold off his equipment, but because it was old, he didn't get much for it. Now he's working for someone else and wondering what went wrong. He never built a system that he could leverage to make himself obsolete.

Another thing to keep in mind when you're thinking about your exit is that your family will probably not want to buy your practice. My kids don't have any interest in becoming dentists, and I didn't have any interest in waiting on them to take over. I sold quite a few practices to the doctors who worked for me over the years, but that's not where the big money is, certainly not compared to exiting through the mergers-and-acquisitions process. Preparing for that will be very different than just selling to an associate.

LUCRATIVE LARRY'S ADVICE ON . . . HIRING AN INVESTMENT BANKER

By now, you should know Dr. Lanier's attitude about doing things yourself—other than being a dentist: Don't do it. An investment banker will cost you, but a good one will make you a lot more money by putting your business in front of the right people, managing negotiations, and getting you a higher price than you would otherwise get. Investment bankers are experts in selling companies, and you're not. Don't blow it at the end; hire a good investment banker and pay the commission. You'll end up richer.

DO

- **Get your business ready to sell.**
- **Build your sales team.**
- **Go through the process.**

It's Time to Sell Your Business!

When you decide that you're ready to exit, there's a lot to do. I like to divide the activities into three categories: "Preparing to Sell," "Gather Your Team," and "Close the Deal." Let's walk through them one at a time.

Preparing to Sell

At this point, you might be talking with an investment banker or just knocking around the idea of selling with your financial advisor or banker. But if you're serious about selling, you'll need to do some prep work. Buyers are after same-store revenue growth, expansion, and a clean operation. You'll need to show that you have cost controls in place to protect strong margins. You'll need clean financials, as we've discussed, so a potential buyer can take a quick look at your books and assess the health of the company. You'll need to switch to accrual accounting if you haven't already, and you'll need a strong brand identity, with a well-designed marketing system generating high awareness and goodwill in the community.

If you've built a business with ten, fifteen, or twenty locations, and it's running smoothly, chances are you have all those things—or can dial them in over the span of a few months. Take your time and prepare your business for the easiest, fastest sale possible. Make sure your financials are clear and transparent; if they make sense to you, they'll make sense to the forensic accountant whose job it is to turn over every stone in your finances and look for problems. If you're running a system-driven business with a strong model and good fundamentals, it will be a desirable property.

There's one more thing to do in preparation: "Obsolete" yourself. Your buyer might want you to stay on and help guide the business for a while after the close, but they won't see you as part of the value proposition. In fact, the more your business depends on your direct intervention to run profitably, the worse it is for you. Months out from initiating the sales process, start backing away from daily operations. Refine your system and processes, document everything with clarity, and make sure your key people know everything you know about running things. You need to be expendable.

Gather Your Team

While all of this is going on, you'll need to put together your all-star team of business-selling superheroes. As I've already discussed, your investment banker is your quarterback. He's the one who will market your company to prospective buyers, help you set a price, solicit and vet bids, and get the deal to closing. But you'll need other people on the team, too.

You'll need a CFO, as I've mentioned, if you don't already have one on your team. Your CFO will move you to an accrual accounting system, work with your CPA to clean up your books, and help you determine your multiple based on all the factors that can affect it.

You'll also need your wealth manager or certified financial planner (CFP) on board. You'll have lots of tax consequences as part of your sale, and you'll need to plan for those. Your financial advisor will assist you with estate planning, setting up foundations to defer some taxes, paying capital gains tax, and other tax-related ways of structuring your deal.

You'll also want a tax attorney on board for similar reasons. You don't want any surprises from the IRS later on to throw cold water on your post-sale celebration.

Close the Deal

Your books are as clean as your treatment rooms. Your systems are documented and your offices hum along without you setting foot in them for days, raking in more than $1 million each per year at a twenty percent margin. You're ready to sell. What happens now?

First, your investment banker will begin soliciting interest from potential buyers: DSOs, private dental companies like yours, and private equity. This can take a few months, but in a category as hot as dental, it probably won't.

In fact, if you've been growing something polished and healthy, you're probably already on someone's short list as an acquisition target.

Once your banker assembles a group of interested potential buyers, he will ask for statements of interest. Potential buyers will deliver formal documents stating their intention to bid on your company. They won't offer numbers yet; they're throwing their hats into the ring and letting you know that they want to be part of the process.

Now comes the nerve-racking part: letting prospective buyers do their due diligence. They will go through your financials, records, and documented processes looking for red flags: debts, potential legal liabilities, unsettled claims on the company, accounting irregularities, and so on. If you and your team have done your work well, you should sail through this part, even though you might feel like you need an antacid.

Once the buyers have done their due diligence, some may bow out of the deal. That's fine. The ones left will be your serious suitors, and at this point, based on their findings, they will submit confidential bids by a deadline set by your investment banker. By the way, you'll be involved in all of this as little as possible; you're too close to it, and you won't want the stress. Trust your banker to collect the offers and move to the next step.

That's where you get involved again: reviewing the bids. You and your team will sit down and go over every bid. At the level you're at, most will be cash, not stock, and some might include the stipulation that you stay on with the company for a time to oversee the switch to new ownership. You'll analyze the bids and may choose to make counteroffers to one or more bidders. At this point, you'll probably also say "Thanks, but no thanks" to some of your suitors.

Now negotiations begin, and your investment banker is in charge of them. He and your final bidders may go back and forth a few times to get you a little more money or sweeten the deal in some way. They'll also tighten up final negotiating points. Eventually, your banker will come to you with a negotiated offer that he feels is in your best interest.

Next is the actual meeting, which you and your team will attend. The buyers will come to you. (We set up meetings in the airport hotel's conference rooms.) One by one, you'll meet with your prospects in all-day meetings. Through this process, you'll thin the herd to the top three, and then you'll agree to sell to one, and you'll sign the paperwork.

In a few weeks, the documents will be approved, the deal will be done, and you'll get your money; you'll pay your investment banker, lawyer, and any shareholders; you'll pay your capital gains taxes—and voilà! You've exited. Now it's time to update your living trust, establish your family foundation, etc. With money comes responsibilities.

Of course, it's not always that quick or easy. But selling doesn't have to be torture, either. It wasn't for me; my buyer was in the dental industry, so they knew how to value what I had built, and the whole thing went pretty smoothly. That's possible if you do your homework and prepare your product to go to market.

TALK TO THE EXPERT 

Investment bankers play a valuable role for dentists considering monetization alternatives. There is never an "exact right time" to sell: Markets change, and the value of a practice can rise and fall rapidly over a relatively short period of time due to reimbursement, overall economic conditions, and the attractiveness of particular practice segments. Therefore, it is essential that practice owners properly plan for the event so that they are best prepared to capture opportunities when the stars are aligned.

continued

This includes making sure financial reporting, compliance, and operational stability are all in good shape. A good investment banker can help an owner prepare for these items and position the practice on a competitive basis, to make sure prospective buyers know there is competition for the practice—even if there is no one else in the arena.

In the case of Kids Dental Kare, Synergy Advisors guided Dr. Jerry Lanier through a successful outcome that resulted in a transaction that nearly doubled what his original expectations were. Here are the steps we took together:

- » We found him a CFO to better present his financial story.
- » We prepared marketing materials that we used in conversations with more than fifty prospective buyers.
- » We ran a rigid sales process, where bidders had to meet our deadlines.
- » We found the buyer that most wanted this practice and was willing to pay for it.
- » We worked with legal counsel to get Dr. Lanier the best possible terms for the sale.

Throughout this process, we had a team surrounding Dr. Lanier for every step. This included legal "deal counsel" (as opposed to general business counsel, who may not know all of the pitfalls of current and future risks in a particular transaction), regulatory advisors (experts on California state dental reimbursement programs), accounting professionals (who needed to defend the financial performance of the business in a "quality of earnings" analysis from an outside accounting firm), and the Synergy Advisors team, who guided all of these parties. Dr. Lanier often found this very intrusive and costly; however, it proved to be well worth it with the success of his exit.

There are numerous practice brokers and investment bankers that specialize in dental practices. Most investment bankers require a minimum of five to ten offices and/or a clear path to grow to that size. Practices below that fall into the purview of practice brokers, many of whom are very good at what they do but take a different approach. As mentioned earlier, it is always best to be prepared, and the right time to meet and potentially engage with an investment banker is often a year before you plan to look for buyers. Sometimes they approach you before you are ready, so early preparation is essential.

—Jim Emslie, Partner, Synergy Advisors[29]

KEEP IN MIND

- **Have your next act in mind.**
- **Make sure you have a good wealth management team.**
- **Mentor others and pay it forward.**

What Now?

I was listening to Tony Robbins the other day, and he said that 87 percent of all businesses will never be sold, because the owners have no exit strategy.[30] That kind of cathartic sale, a validation of everything you've built and all your hard work and sacrifice, is something few people experience. If you

29 Email interview, September 24, 2018.

30 Tony Robbins, "What's Your Exit Strategy?," Tony Robbins Business Mastery (video), October 11, 2017, https://www.youtube.com/watch?time_continue=2&v=K4CaG_lRK18.

have the good fortune to experience it, let me tell you that it will be one of the high points of your life. When it comes, savor it.

But then what? What do you do when the money's in the bank, more money than you'll need to last you for the rest of your life, and you don't need to go to the office anymore? Some dentists actually struggle with this and try to stay involved in the profession. Not me. I actually let the state put my license on inactive status. I'm done. If I ever needed to, I could take some continuing education courses and make a comeback, but I don't intend to do that. I'm going forward. Hopefully, next year I'll be wealthier than I am today, and ten years from now, wealthier still. I'm moving into what Robert Kiyosaki calls the *investor quadrant*.

I've had a vision for my post-exit life for a while, but not all dentists do. We're so obsessed with growing the business, and then with selling it, that when the deal finally closes and the party is over, we find ourselves standing there saying, "What happened?" I've actually known colleagues who, despite walking away with millions, were depressed and unhappy because they didn't know what to do with their time.

We all need a purpose, a reason to get up in the morning. As Art Linkletter used to say, the number one killer of old people is retirement. You need to work at something, even if it's not building a dental office and managing associates half your age. So as you think about growing your business and making an exit, even if it's ten years in the future, ask yourself, "What does my next act look like?"

One thing I suggest it *not* look like: sitting on your backside. You've worked for years; it's in your blood. If you don't want to build another dental business, that's probably healthy. It's good to let go of what you had and move forward. Too many dentists get hung up on staying associated with what they built and can't let go. It's time to let someone else run things. Take the cash and know that if you built something great once, you can do it again. It doesn't even have to be in the world of dentistry. You can build other things, now that you know what you know, and do it over and over again.

Yes, after you exit, you should play some golf. Travel. Kick back. Enjoy the good life. But don't get too used to it, because that's not how you're wired. I know, because I'm like you. We're workers. We're entrepreneurs. That doesn't end when you sell. It just means you have more time and resources to go in new directions. This book is part of my new direction. In fact, it's going to be hard for me not to make even more money than I already have, because now I have all of this knowledge. I finally see why the rich get richer, because now you know how to build things of value. You say, "That wasn't too hard, and with what I've learned, I can do it again, but faster." You keep moving. That's what entrepreneurs do.

Have a vision for your post-exit life. What does it look like? How will you spend your time? Who will you spend it with? What will give your days meaning? What will you look forward to? What will push you and challenge you? Will you go back to school? Start a new business? Write a book? Train for a marathon? Teach? Sit on a board of directors?

Make Friends with a Wealth Manager

Whatever your post-exit picture looks like, make sure a wealth manager is part of it, because the financial complications don't end when your sale closes. You'll have tax obligations. New classes of investments will be open to you, such as hedge funds. Estate planning, tax-free gifts—it will all become more important, now that you have more assets to protect.

Make sure your wealth manager is accredited either as a CFP or an RIA (registered investment advisor). That ensures that he or she is well trained and highly qualified to help you manage your post-exit financial life, whether that means reducing taxes and starting a charitable foundation or buying real estate and starting another business. Consider hiring someone with an office full of people who can manage every aspect of your financial life, from paying bills to making donations, so you don't have to worry about it.

Finally, find a way to give back to other people. You owe a debt to the people who helped you make a successful journey, and if you can't repay them personally, you can mentor other dentists and entrepreneurs so they can enjoy the incredible potential of this profession. While I was learning to scuba dive, I also gave a lot of money to my alma mater. I launched my Entrepreneur Dentist program to teach people what I learned and help them avoid the mistakes that served as my personal classroom.

Now that you have money, you have a responsibility to use your time and experience to lift others up. You could go out and buy a couple of Bentleys and a bigger house, and spend money on stupid things, but not me. I want to help kids. One of my doctors, when I was trying to write articles and inspire people, said to me, "That's the way. Pay it forward, Doc." I was proud of that then, and I still am. The guys that mentored me are gone, but I can step into their shoes and help others, so that's what I'm doing.

Find *what* you care about, and *who* you care about, and make a difference when you can, even if you haven't made your exit yet. Life isn't all about work and money. It's about people and hope. Never forget that.

Every Successful Entrepreneur Fails, Too

One last thing before I go, because I know you have work to do. I've painted this rosy picture (mostly) of my rise from North Carolina farm boy to wealthy retired dental entrepreneur, but I didn't know what I was doing all the time. I made a lot of mistakes that, looking back, were just dumb. But that's what entrepreneurs do. We take risks, and with risk comes failure. If you're not failing from time to time, you're not taking enough risks to build something worth buying.

I have never known of a single successful entrepreneur who hasn't tasted failure at some time. You will too, so be a proud member of the club. We're the movers and shakers of the world, the people who are not content to stay still. We test the waters. We go out on a limb. We would rather try and fail than never try in the first place. So we make bad calls, hire the wrong person, trust someone we shouldn't, or let our egos get the best of us. What makes us entrepreneurs is that after we get knocked down, we get back up, say, "That was a valuable lesson," and keep going.

My failures occurred when I strayed from my niche. Sometimes I'd be so intent on making something work out that I would work harder and harder; what I really needed to do was refocus and concentrate on my niche. I always found that when I got back on track, things turned around. I also learned that sometimes I would have been better off listening to others and not only to myself all the time. My second wife became one of my greatest assets, both personally and professionally, because she's a lot smarter than I am.

As you build your dental business and grow it into something saleable, plan to fail. Count on it. If you're not failing, you're not testing the waters. Open the extra office, even though it scares the daylights out of you. Invest in expensive marketing. Hire someone brilliant but hard to manage and learn to be a leader. Push yourself. Venture into uncharted territory. Innovate. If you fail, lose money, or embarrass yourself, keep going. This can be an incredible business. Now go build one of your own.

EYEING THE EXIT

Your exit team will guide you to a successful sale, but your post-exit life is up to nobody but you. You need to have a plan in mind for your next act. I chose to build Entrepreneur Dentist to mentor young dentists and help them build valuable franchises. This gives me a new purpose, while also helping me leverage my time and knowledge to create a new income stream. But that's far from your only post-exit option. You could—

- » Invest in dental businesses. Use your vast experience to guide growing practices, and even step in as a fractional COO.
- » Build a completely different kind of business. If you've always had a burning interest in something that has nothing to do with dentistry, this might be your chance to turn it into something. The great thing is, because you're rich now, if the new venture flops, it's no big deal.
- » Get into charitable work. Sit on boards, give to health-related nonprofits, and even volunteer to work in mobile dental clinics serving low-income areas.
- » Teach. Inquire with dental schools or organizations like the ADSO about lecturing, conducting seminars, or actually teaching classes in dentistry—or the business of running a dental practice.

The only limits here are your imagination, time, and commitment.

Index

C

G

H

I

R

T

U

V

W

Z

About the Author

DR. LANIER IS AN ENTREPRENEUR DENTIST WHO FOUNDED KIDS Dental Kare and sold it to Western Dental Services, Inc. in 2017. He built twenty-six *de novo* offices as 100 percent owner. His emphasis is on dentists building a franchise-like brand and devising an exit strategy focusing on EBITDA. As an investor, he is now involved in TKO Dental Properties, LLC, and MKTGdocs.com.

Dr. Lanier has dedicated many hours to clinical dentistry, mostly in underserved areas. After leaving Meharry Dental School, in Nashville, TN, he served for four years in the U.S. Public Health Service Corps in New Orleans, LA. He relocated to Los Angeles in 1991 and founded Kids Dental Kare in 1994. Dr. Lanier received an Executive MBA from UCLA, Anderson School, in 2006. He has studied under Michael Gerber and various success coaches like Jim Rohn and Anthony Robbins.

Mentoring and simplifying business for dentists is Dr. Lanier's mission. He coined the phrase "If your money stops every time you stop, you need to get a better plan." He now has time to enjoy playing jazz and being with family, thanks to his rags-to-riches story that has ended in a great exit.